EUROPEAN POCKET EDITION

SIXTH EDITION

Exclusive Distributors:
Hal Leonard Europe
1 Red Place
London W1K 6PL
Email: info@halleonardeurope.com

Order No. HLE90003232
ISBN 13: 978-1-84772-081-8
This book © Copyright 2007 by Hal Leonard Europe

For all works contained herein:
Unauthorized copying, arranging, adapting, recording, Internet posting, public performance,
or other distribution of the music in this publication is an infringement of copyright.
Infringers are liable under the law.

Printed in China

This publication is not authorised for sale in
the United States of America and/or Canada

HAL LEONARD EUROPE

PREFACE

The Real Book is the answer to the fake book. It is an alternative to the plethora of poorly designed, illegible, inaccurate, badly edited volumes which abound on the market today. The Real Book is extremely accurate, neat, and is designed, above all, for practical use. Every effort has been made to make it enjoyable to play. Here are some of the primary features:

1. FORMAT
    a. The book is professionally copied and meticulously checked for accuracy in melody, harmony, and rhythms.
    b. Form within each tune, including both phrases and larger sections, is clearly delineated and placed in obvious visual arrangement.
    c. All two-page tunes open to face one another.
    d. Most standard-type tunes remain true to their original harmonies with little or no reharmonization. The exceptions include a handful of jazz interpretations of popular songs and Broadway showtunes, as well as some modifications using modern notation and variation among turnarounds.

2. SELECTION OF TUNES AND EDITING
    a. Major jazz composers of the last 60 years are highlighted, with special attention given to the 1960s and 1970s.
    b. While some commonly played tunes are absent from the book, many of the classics are here, including bop standards and a fine selection of Duke Ellington masterpieces.
    c. Many of the included arrangements represent the work of the jazz giants of the last 40 years – Miles, Coltrane, Shorter, Hancock, Evans, Mingus, and Monk, as well as a variety of newer artists.
    d. A variety of recordings and alternate editions were consulted to create the most accurate and user-friendly representations of the tunes, whether used in a combo setting or as a solo artist.

3. SOURCE REFERENCE
    a. The composer(s) of every tune is listed.
    b. Every song presented in the Real Book is now fully licensed for use.

Sixth Edition
As we ventured into the 21st century, the same Real Book that has served us so faithfully for the last 30 years was in need of a facelift. This new edition contains tunes that are re-arranged, re-transcribed and most importantly, licensed, so that you may study and play these works more accurately and legally. Enjoy!

A

AFTERNOON IN PARIS 6
ÁGUA DE BEBER
(WATER TO DRINK) 8
AIN'T MISBEHAVIN' 7
AIN'T THAT A KICK IN THE HEAD 10
AIREGIN 11
ALFIE 12
ALICE IN WONDERLAND 13
ALL BLUES 14
ALL BY MYSELF 15
ALL OR NOTHING AT ALL 16
ALL THE THINGS YOU ARE 18
ALL THE WAY 19
ALRIGHT, OKAY, YOU WIN 20
AMOR 22
ANA MARIA 24
ANGEL EYES 26
ANTHROPOLOGY 27
ANTIGUA 28
APRIL JOY 30
AREN'T YOU GLAD YOU'RE YOU 31
ARISE, HER EYES 32
ARMAGEDDON 34
AS LONG AS I LIVE 35
AU PRIVAVE 36

B

BARK FOR BARKSDALE 37
BEAUTY AND THE BEAST 38
BERNIE'S TUNE 39
BÉSAME MUCHO (KISS ME MUCH) .. 40
BESSIE'S BLUES 42
BETWEEN THE DEVIL
AND THE DEEP BLUE SEA 43
BEYOND THE BLUE HORIZON 44
BIG NICK 45
BLACK COFFEE 46
BLACK NILE 47
BLACK ORPHEUS 48
BLACKBERRY WINTER 49
BLUE BOSSA 50
BLUE CHAMPAGNE 51
BLUE IN GREEN 52
BLUE MONK 53
BLUES FOR ALICE 54

BLUESETTE 55
BOPLICITY 56
BRAZIL 58
BUD POWELL 60
BUTTERFLY 57
BYE BYE BABY 62
BYRD LIKE 63

C

CALL ME 64
CALL ME IRRESPONSIBLE 65
CAN'T HELP LOVIN' DAT MAN 66
CAPTAIN MARVEL 68
CELIA 67
CENTRAL PARK WEST 70
CHEGA DE SAUDADE
(NO MORE BLUES) 72
CHELSEA BELLS 71
CHELSEA BRIDGE 74
A CHILD IS BORN 75
CHIPPIE 76
CHITLINS CON CARNE 77
COME FLY WITH ME 78
COME SUNDAY 80
COMO EN VIETNAM 81
CONFIRMATION 82
CONTEMPLATION 83
COUNTDOWN 84
CRAZY 86
CRESCENT 85
CRYSTAL SILENCE 88

D

D NATURAL BLUES 89
DAAHOUD 90
DAY WAVES 92
DEAR OLD STOCKHOLM 93
DEARLY BELOVED 94
DEDICATED TO YOU 95
DELUGE 96
DESAFINADO 98
DESERT AIR 100
DEXTERITY 102
DIG 103
DIZZY ATMOSPHERE 104
DJANGO 106
DOIN' THE PIG 108
DOLORES 105
DOLPHIN DANCE 110
DOMINO BISCUIT 111
DON'T BLAME ME 112
DON'T GET AROUND
MUCH ANYMORE 113
DON'T KNOW WHY 114
DREAMSVILLE 115

E

EAST OF THE SUN 116
EASY LIVING 117
ECCLUSIASTICS 118
EIGHTY ONE 119
EL GAUCHO 120
THE END OF A LOVE AFFAIR 121
EPISTROPHY 122
EQUINOX 123
EQUIPOISE 124
E.S.P. 125
EVERYTHING HAPPENS TO ME 126
EXACTLY LIKE YOU 127

F

THE FACE I LOVE 128
FALL 129
FALLING GRACE 130
FALLING IN LOVE AGAIN 131
FEE-FI-FO-FUM 132
FINE AND MELLOW 134
A FINE ROMANCE 133
500 MILES HIGH 136
502 BLUES 137
FOLLOW YOUR HEART 138
FOOTPRINTS 139
FOR ALL WE KNOW 140
FOR EVERY MAN
THERE'S A WOMAN 141
FOR HEAVEN'S SAKE 142
FOREST FLOWER 143
FOUR 144
FOUR ON SIX 145
FREDDIE FREELOADER 146
FREEDOM JAZZ DANCE 147
FULL HOUSE 148

G

GEE BABY, AIN'T I GOOD TO YOU .. 150
GEMINI 151
GET HAPPY 152
GIANT STEPS 153
THE GIRL FROM IPANEMA 154
GLORIA'S STEP 155
GOD BLESS' THE CHILD 156
GOOD EVENING
MR. AND MRS. AMERICA 158
GOOD MORNING HEARTACHE 157
GOT A MATCH? 160
GRAND CENTRAL 161
THE GREEN MOUNTAINS 162
GROOVIN' HIGH 163

H

HEART AND SOUL	164
HEEBIE JEEBIES	165
HELLO, YOUNG LOVERS	166
HERE'S THAT RAINY DAY	168
HIGH HOPES	169
HOT TODDY	170
HOUSE OF JADE	171
HOW INSENSITIVE	172
HOW MY HEART SINGS	173
HULLO BOLINAS	174

I

I AIN'T GOT NOBODY	175
I CAN'T GIVE YOU ANYTHING BUT LOVE	176
I DON'T KNOW WHY	177
I DON'T WANT TO WALK WITHOUT YOU	178
I FOUND A MILLION DOLLAR BABY	179
I HEAR MUSIC	180
I KEEP GOING BACK TO JOE'S	181
I MEAN YOU	182
I REMEMBER CLIFFORD	184
I SHOULD CARE	183
I WANNA BE LOVED	186
I WISH I KNEW HOW IT WOULD FEEL TO BE FREE	187
I WISHED ON THE MOON	188
I WON'T DANCE	190
I'LL BE AROUND	189
I'LL BE SEEING YOU	192
I'LL GET BY	193
I'LL NEVER SMILE AGAIN	194
I'LL REMEMBER APRIL	195
I'M ALWAYS CHASING RAINBOWS	196
I'M BEGINNING TO SEE THE LIGHT	197
I'M OLD FASHIONED	198
I'M YOUR PAL	199
I'VE GOT THE WORLD ON A STRING	200
I'VE NEVER BEEN IN LOVE BEFORE	201
ICARUS	202
IF YOU NEVER COME TO ME	204
ILL WIND	205
IMPRESSIONS	206
IN LOVE IN VAIN	207
IN THE COOL, COOL, COOL OF THE EVENING	208
IN THE WEE SMALL HOURS OF THE MORNING	209
THE INCH WORM	210
INDIAN LADY	211
INTERPLAY	212
THE INTREPID FOX	213
INVITATION	214
IRIS	215
IS YOU IS, OR IS YOU AIN'T (MA' BABY)	216
ISN'T IT ROMANTIC?	218
ISRAEL	219
IT'S A BIG WIDE WONDERFUL WORLD	220
IT'S EASY TO REMEMBER	221
IT'S SO NICE TO HAVE A MAN AROUND THE HOUSE	222

J

JELLY ROLL	223
THE JIVE SAMBA	224
JORDU	225
JOURNEY TO RECIFE	226
JOY SPRING	227
JUJU	228
JUMP MONK	230
JUNE IN JANUARY	229
JUST ONE MORE CHANCE	232

K

KELO	234

L

LADY BIRD	233
LADY SINGS THE BLUES	236
THE LADY'S IN LOVE WITH YOU	237
LAS VEGAS TANGO	238
LAZY BIRD	239
LAZY RIVER	240
LET'S GET AWAY FROM IT ALL	241
LINE FOR LYONS	242
LINES AND SPACES	244
LITHA	246
LITTLE BOAT	243
LITTLE GIRL BLUE	248
LITTLE WALTZ	249
LONG AGO (AND FAR AWAY)	250
LONNIE'S LAMENT	251
LOVE LETTERS	252
LULLABY OF BIRDLAND	253
LUSH LIFE	254

M

MAHJONG	256
MAIDEN VOYAGE	257
A MAN AND A WOMAN	258
MAN IN THE GREEN SHIRT	260
MAS QUE NADA	262
MAYBE I SHOULD CHANGE MY WAYS	263
THE MEANING OF THE BLUES	264
MEDITATION	265
MICHELLE	266
MIDNIGHT MOOD	267
MIDWESTERN NIGHTS DREAM	268
MILANO	270
MIMI	271
MISS ANN	272
MISSOURI UNCOMPROMISED	273
MR. P.C.	274
MISTY	275
MIYAKO	276
MONA LISA	277
MOON AND SAND	278
MOONLIGHT BECOMES YOU	279
MORE I CANNOT WISH YOU	280
MY BUDDY	282
MY FAVORITE THINGS	283
MY IDEAL	284
MY SILENT LOVE	285
MY WAY	286
MYSTERIOUS TRAVELLER	288

N

NAIMA	287
NANCY - WITH THE LAUGHING FACE	290
NARDIS	291
NEFERTITI	292
NEVER LET ME GO	293
NEVER WILL I MARRY	294
NIGHT DREAMER	295
THE NIGHT HAS A THOUSAND EYES	296
A NIGHT IN TUNISIA	297
NIGHT TRAIN	298
THE NIGHT WE CALLED IT A DAY	300
NO MOON AT ALL	301
NOBODY ELSE BUT ME	302
NOBODY KNOWS YOU WHEN YOU'RE DOWN AND OUT	303
NOSTALGIA IN TIMES SQUARE	304

O

(OLD MAN FROM) THE OLD COUNTRY	305
OLEO	306
OLILOQUI VALLEY	307
ON A SLOW BOAT TO CHINA	308
ONCE I LOVED	309
ONCE IN LOVE WITH AMY	310
ONE FINGER SNAP	311
ONE NOTE SAMBA	312
ONLY TRUST YOUR HEART	313
ORBITS	314
ORNITHOLOGY	315
OUT OF NOWHERE	316

P

Title	Page
PAPER DOLL	317
PASSION DANCE	318
PEACE	319
PEGGY'S BLUE SKYLIGHT	320
PENT UP HOUSE	321
PENTHOUSE SERENADE	322
PERI'S SCOPE	323
PFRANCING (NO BLUES)	324
PINOCCHIO	325
PITHECANTHROPUS ERECTUS	326
PORTSMOUTH FIGURATIONS	327
PRELUDE TO A KISS	328
PRETEND	329
PRINCE OF DARKNESS	330
P.S. I LOVE YOU	331
PURE IMAGINATION	332
PUSSY CAT DUES	333
PUT ON A HAPPY FACE	334

Q

Title	Page
QUIET NIGHTS OF QUIET STARS	335
QUIET NOW	336
QUIZÁS, QUIZÁS, QUIZÁS (PERHAPS, PERHAPS, PERHAPS)	337

R

Title	Page
RED CLAY	338
RED TOP	340
REFLECTIONS	341
REINCARNATION OF A LOVEBIRD	342
ROAD SONG	344
ROCKIN' CHAIR	345
RUBY, MY DEAR	346

S

Title	Page
THE SAGA OF HARRISON CRABFEATHERS	348
SATIN DOLL	349
SCOTCH AND SODA	350
SCRAPPLE FROM THE APPLE	351
SEA JOURNEY	352
SEVEN STEPS TO HEAVEN	354
SHAWNUFF	356
SIDEWINDER	357
SILVER HOLLOW	358
SIRABHORN	359
SISTER SADIE	360
SKATING IN CENTRAL PARK	362
SMALL FRY	361
SO NICE (SUMMER SAMBA)	364
SO WHAT	366
SOLAR	365
SOME DAY MY PRINCE WILL COME	368
SOME OTHER SPRING	369
SOME SKUNK FUNK	370
SOMEBODY LOVES ME	372
SONG FOR MY FATHER	373
THE SONG IS YOU	374
SONG OF THE JET	376
SOPHISTICATED LADY	378
THE SORCERER	379
SPEAK NO EVIL	380
THE SPHINX	381
STANDING ON THE CORNER	382
THE STAR-CROSSED LOVERS	383
STELLA BY STARLIGHT	384
STEPS	385
STOLEN MOMENTS	386
STRAIGHT NO CHASER	387
STUFF	388
A SUNDAY KIND OF LOVE	390
THE SURREY WITH THE FRINGE ON TOP	391
SWEET GEORGIA BRIGHT	392
SWEET HENRY	393

T

Title	Page
TAKE FIVE	394
TAKE THE "A" TRAIN	395
TAME THY PEN	396
TEACH ME TONIGHT	398
TELL ME A BEDTIME STORY	400
THANKS FOR THE MEMORY	399
THAT OLD BLACK MAGIC	402
THAT OLD FEELING	404
THAT'S AMORE	406
THERE'LL BE SOME CHANGES MADE	405
THEY DIDN'T BELIEVE ME	408
THINGS AIN'T WHAT THEY USED TO BE	409
THINK ON ME	410
THREE FLOWERS	411
TIME REMEMBERED	412
TONES FOR JOAN'S BONES	413
TOPSY	414
TOUR DE FORCE	415
TRISTE	416
TUNE UP	417
TURN OUT THE STARS	418
TWISTED BLUES	419

U

Title	Page
UNCHAIN MY HEART	420
UNIQUITY ROAD	422
UNITY VILLAGE	423
UP JUMPED SPRING	424
UPPER MANHATTAN MEDICAL GROUP	425

V

Title	Page
VALSE HOT	426
VERY EARLY	427
THE VERY THOUGHT OF YOU	428
VIOLETS FOR YOUR FURS	429
VIRGO	430

W

Title	Page
WALTZ FOR DEBBY	432
WATERMELON MAN	431
WAVE	434
WE'LL BE TOGETHER AGAIN	435
WELL YOU NEEDN'T	436
WEST COAST BLUES	437
WHAT I DID FOR LOVE	438
WHAT WAS	439
WHEN SUNNY GETS BLUE	440
WHILE WE'RE YOUNG	442
WHISPERING	441
WHY TRY TO CHANGE ME NOW	444
WILD FLOWER	446
WINDOWS	445
WITCH HUNT	448
WITH EVERY BREATH I TAKE	449
WIVES AND LOVERS	450
WOODCHOPPER'S BALL	452
THE WORLD IS WAITING FOR THE SUNRISE	453

Y

Title	Page
YES AND NO	454
YES INDEED	455
YESTERDAY	456
YESTERDAYS	457
YOU BELONG TO MY HEART	458
YOU BROUGHT A NEW KIND OF LOVE TO ME	459
YOU DON'T KNOW WHAT LOVE IS	460
YOU'RE MINE YOU	461
YOU'VE CHANGED	462
YOUNG AT HEART	463
YOUNGER THAN SPRINGTIME	464

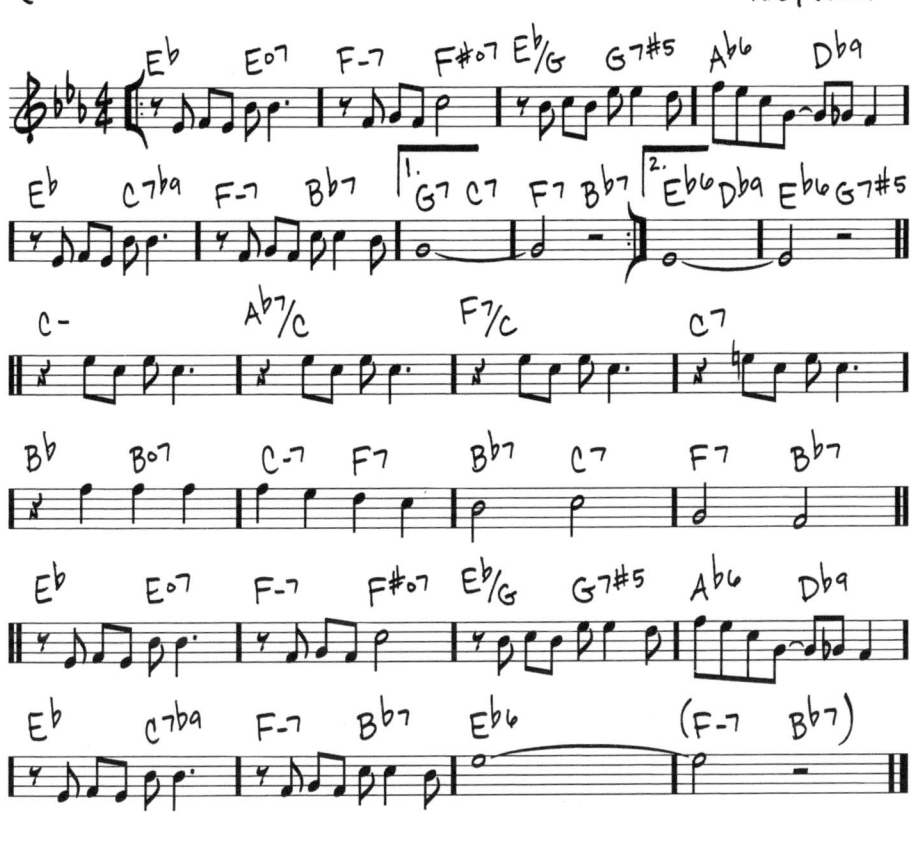

Ain't That a Kick in the Head

— James Van Heusen / Sammy Cahn

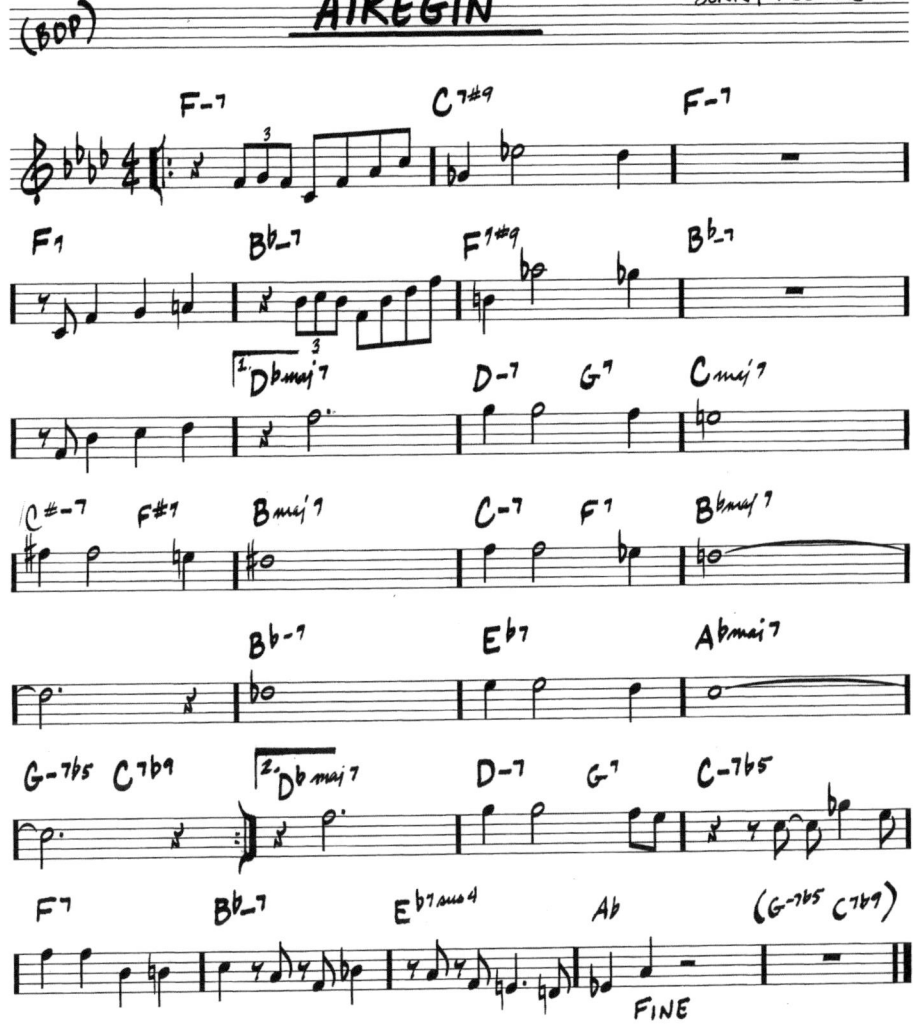

Alice in Wonderland

— Sammy Fain / Bob Hilliard

(Med.)

| D-7 | G7 | Cmaj7 | Fmaj7 | B-7b5 | E7 |

| A-7 | Eb7 | D-7 | G7 | E-7 | A-7 |

| D-7 | G7 | 1. E-7 | A7 | 2. Cmaj7 | A7 |

| D7 | G7 | E-7 | A-7 | D-7 | |

| G7 | Cmaj7 | Fmaj7 | F#-7b5 | B7b9 | |

| E-7 | A7 | D-7 | A7 | D-7 | A7 | D-7 | Ab7 | G7 |

| D-7 | G7 | Cmaj7 | Fmaj7 | B-7b5 | |

| E7 | A-7 | Eb7 | D-7 | G7 | |

| E-7 | A-7 | D-7 | G7 | Cmaj7 | |

FINE

(MED. LATIN)

AMOR
(AMOR, AMOR, AMOR)

– GABRIEL RUIZ/
RICARDO LOPEZ MENDEZ/
NORMAN NEWELL

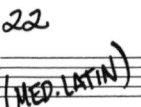

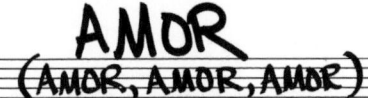

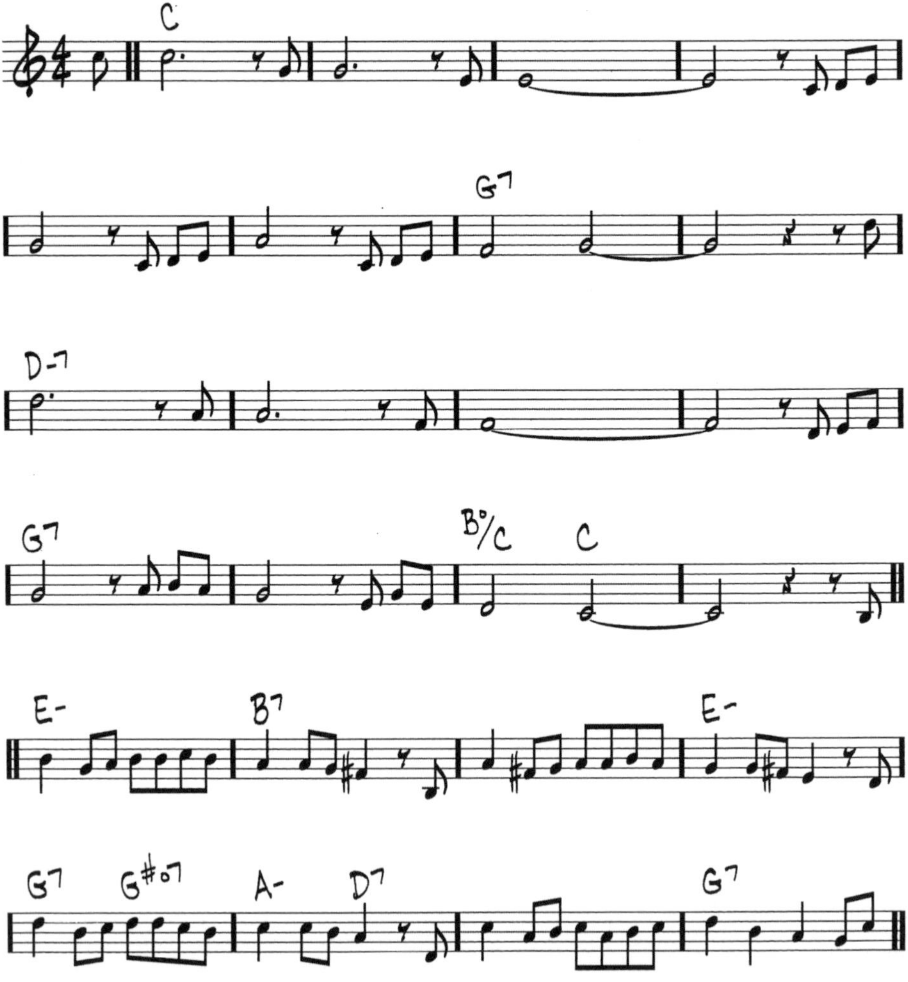

Copyright © 1941,1943 by Promotora Hispano Americana de Musica, S.A.
Copyrights Renewed
All Rights Administered by Peer International Corporation

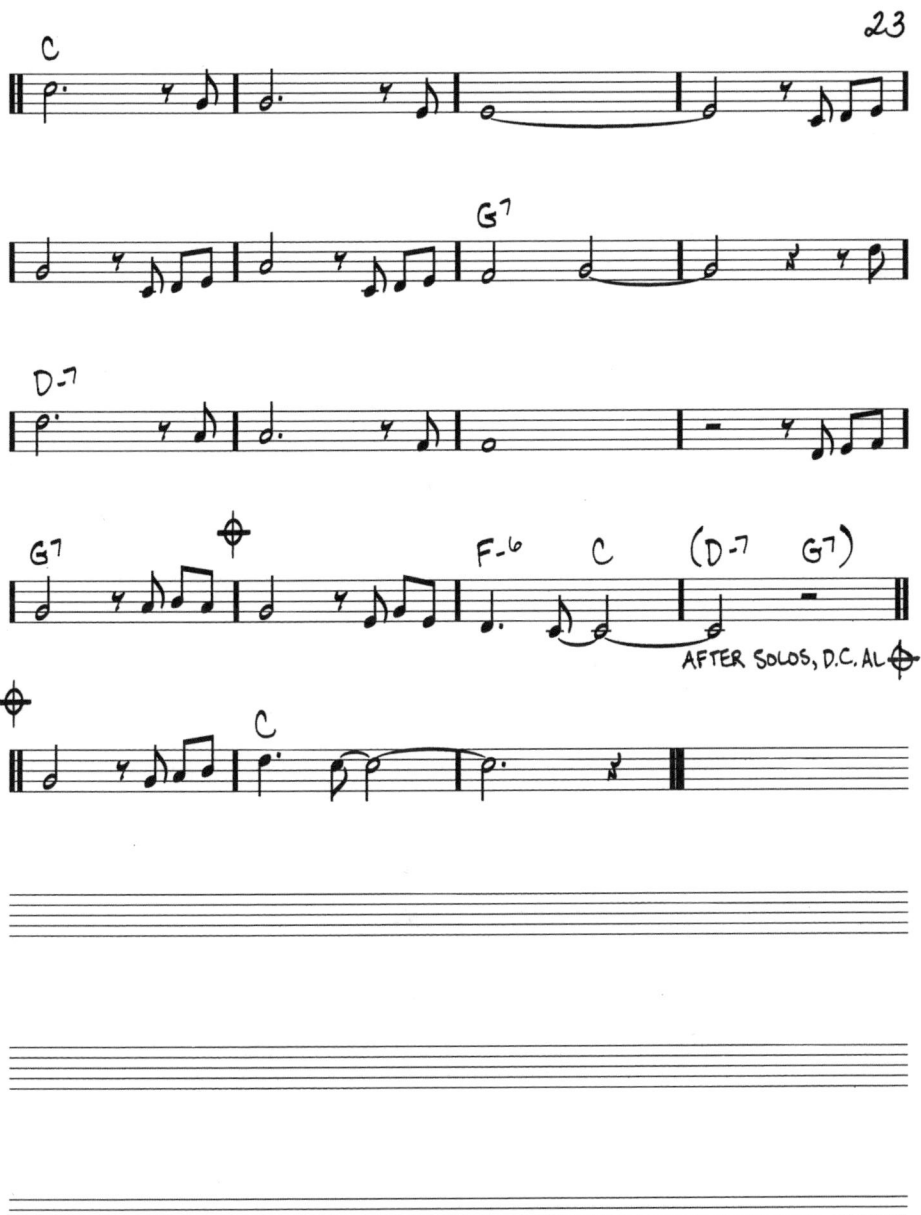

ANTIGUA

(MED. BOSSA)

- ANTONIO CARLOS JOBIM

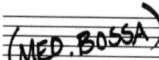

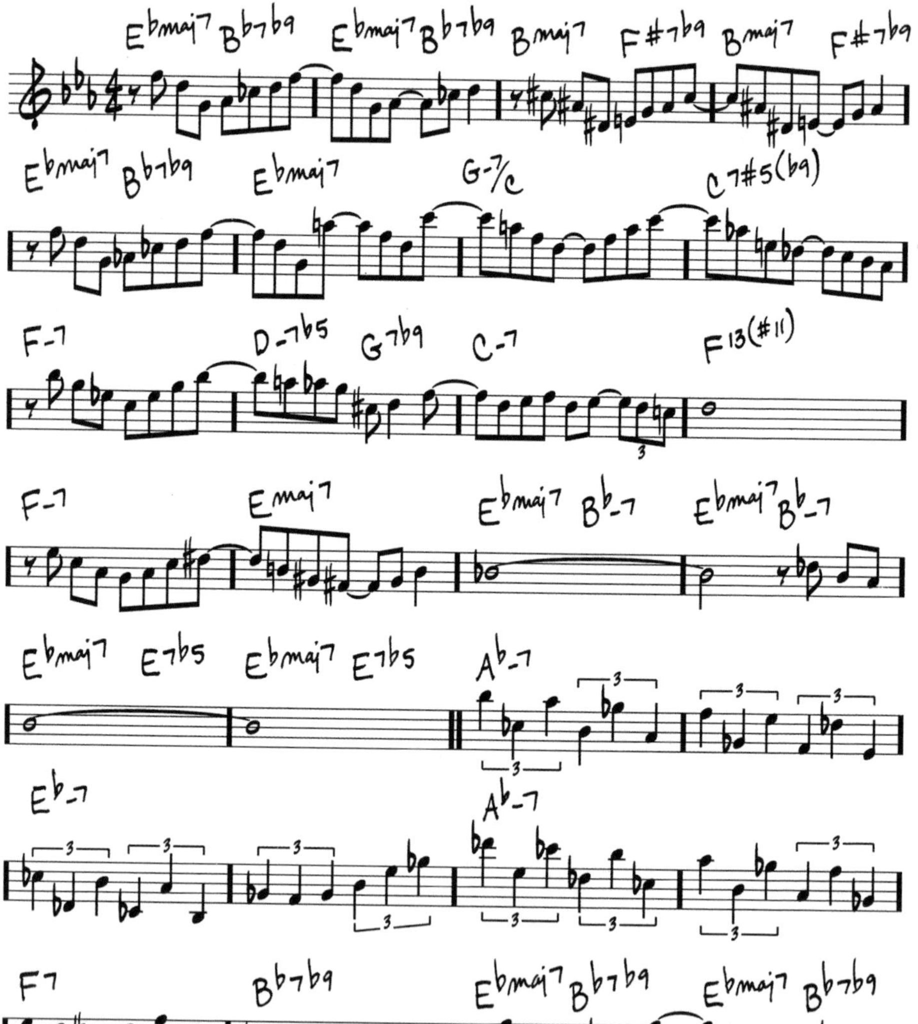

Copyright © 1967, 1968 Antonio Carlos Jobim
Copyright Renewed
Published by Corcovado Music Corp.

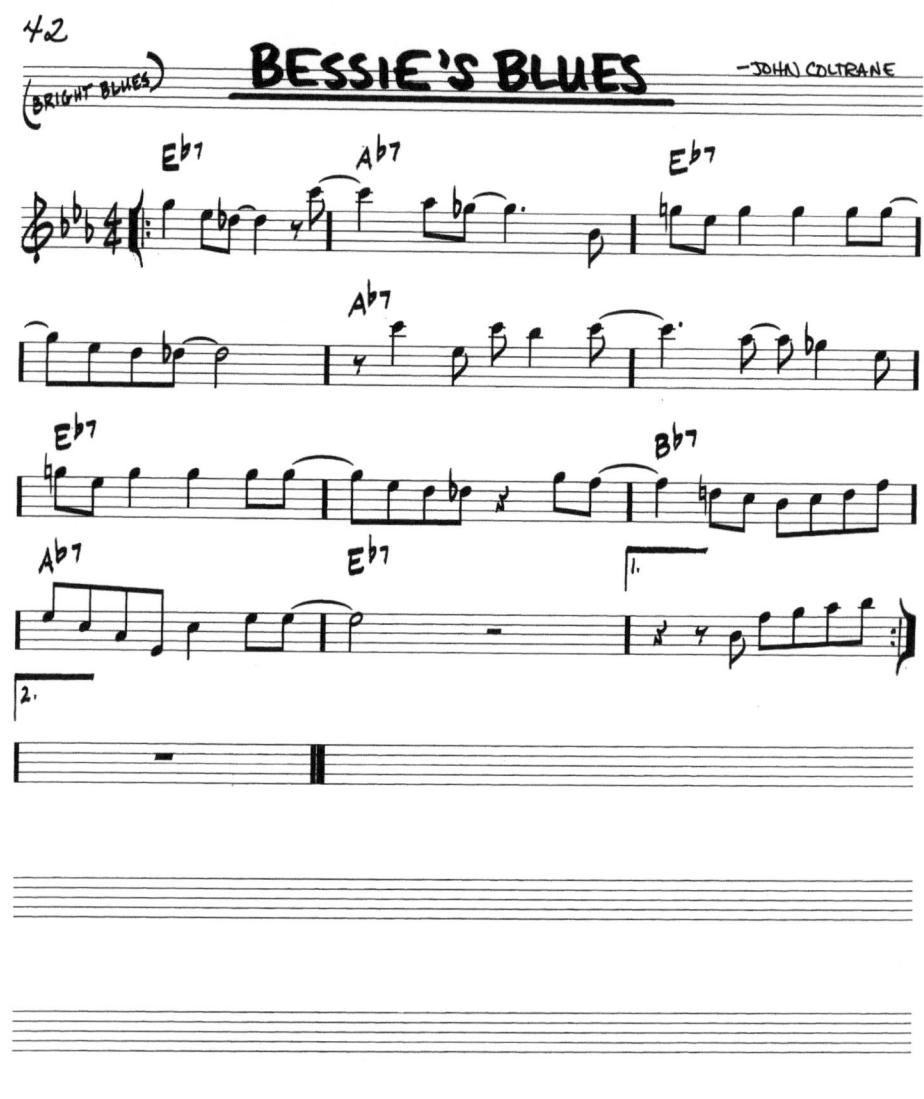

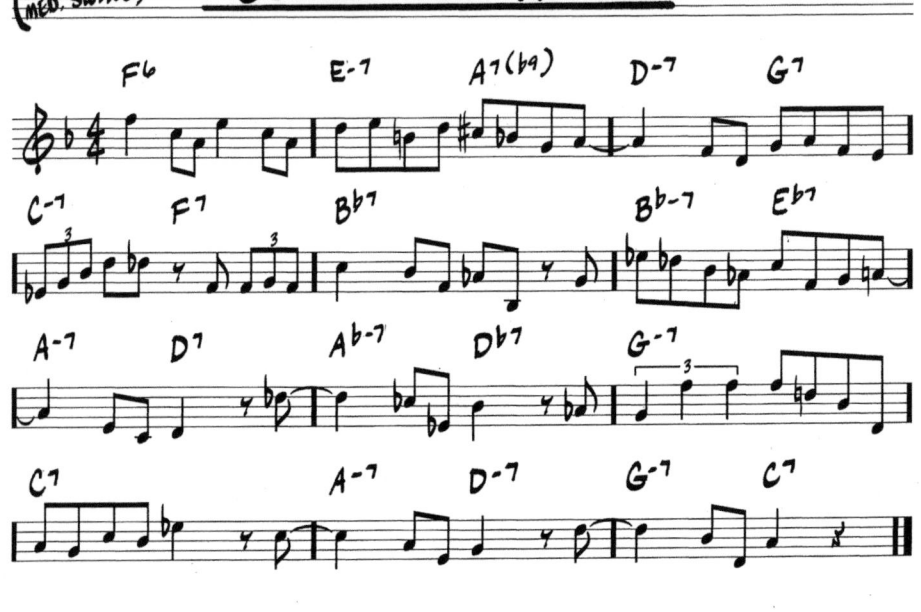

CALL ME
— Tony Hatch

Can't Help Lovin' Dat Man

(Ballad or Med.) — Jerome Kern / Oscar Hammerstein II

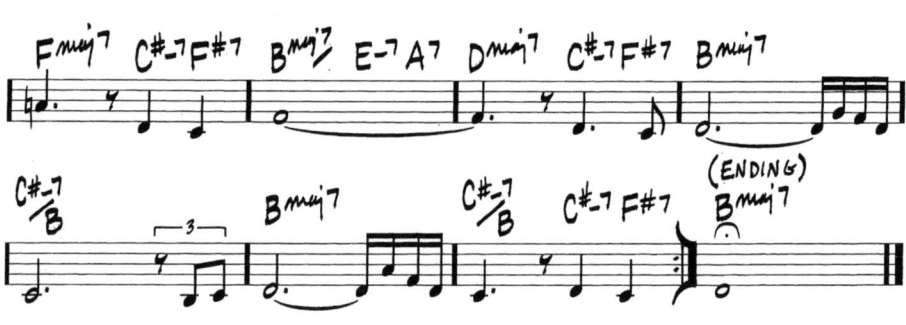

(LATIN BLUES)

CHITLINS CON CARNE

-KENNY BURRELL

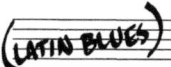

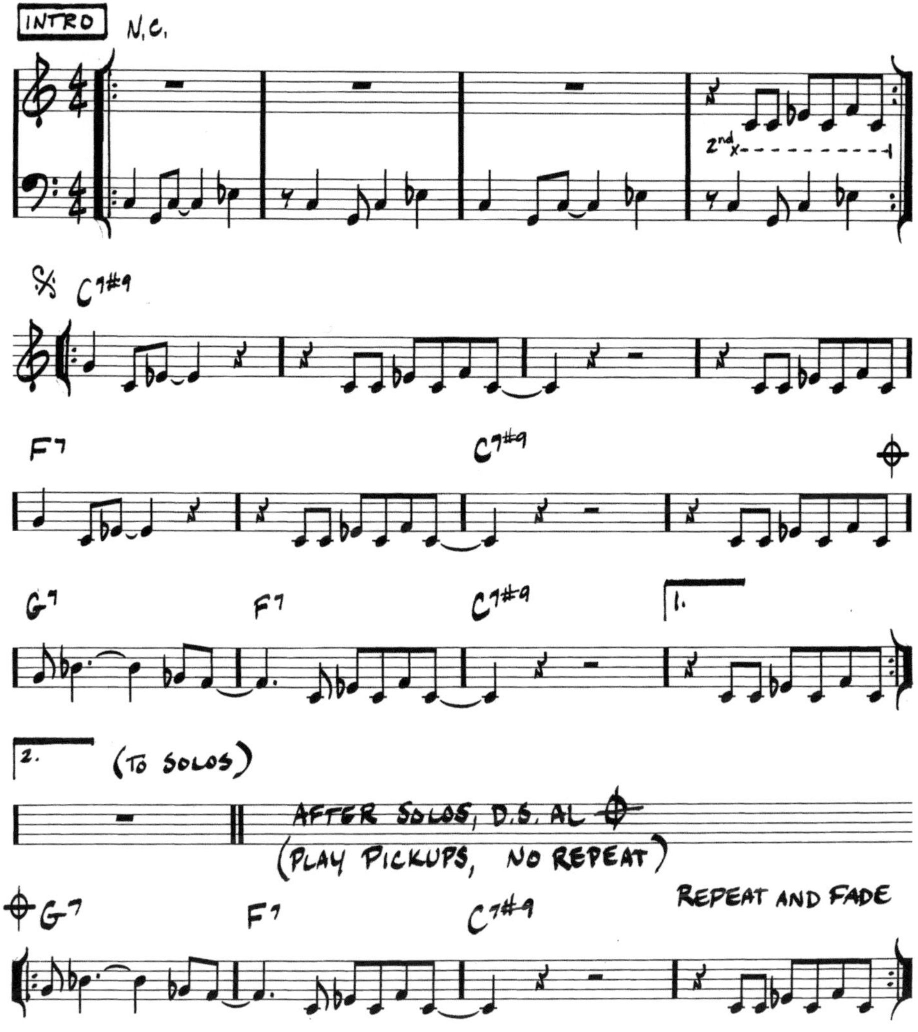

Copyright © 1963 (Renewed 1991) by Elliot Music Co., Inc.

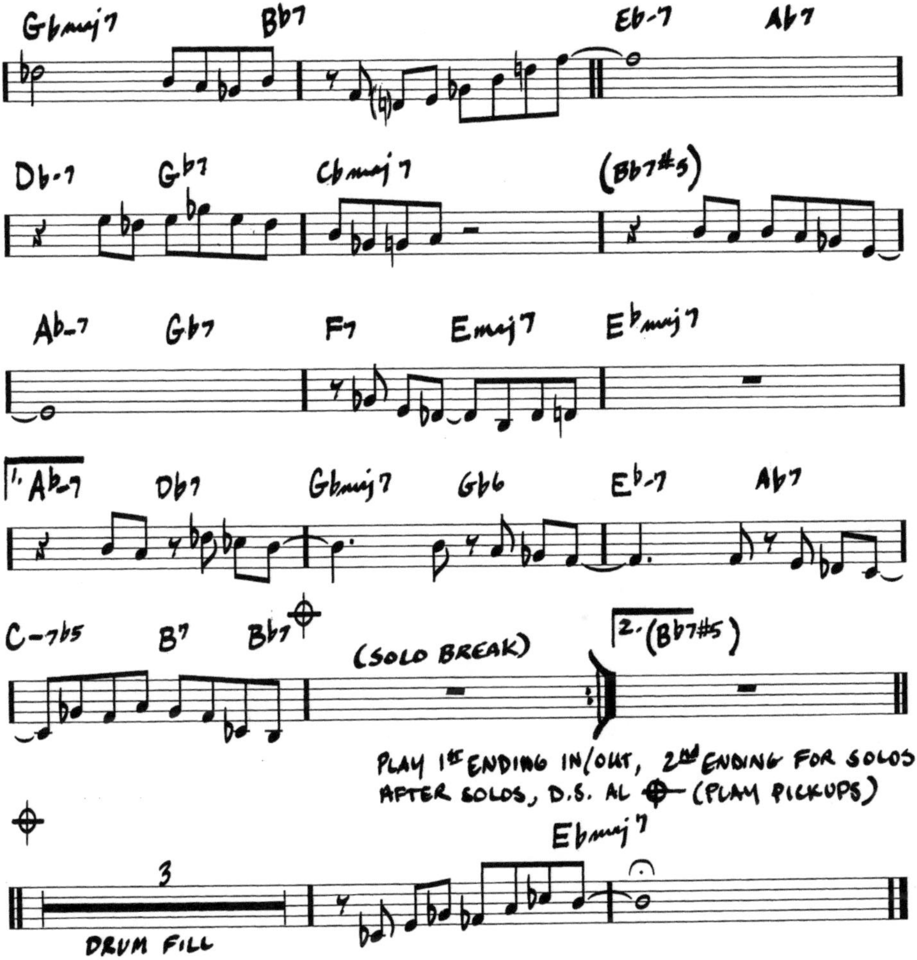

Gbmaj7 Bb7 Eb-7 Ab7
Db-7 Gb7 Cbmaj7 (Bb7#5)
Ab-7 Gb7 F7 Emaj7 Ebmaj7
1. Ab-7 Db7 Gbmaj7 Gb6 Eb-7 Ab7
C-7b5 B7 Bb7
(SOLO BREAK)
2. (Bb7#5)
PLAY 1st ENDING IN/OUT, 2nd ENDING FOR SOLOS
AFTER SOLOS, D.S. AL ⊕ (PLAY PICKUPS)
Ebmaj7
3
DRUM FILL

DEAR OLD STOCKHOLM

—VARMELAND

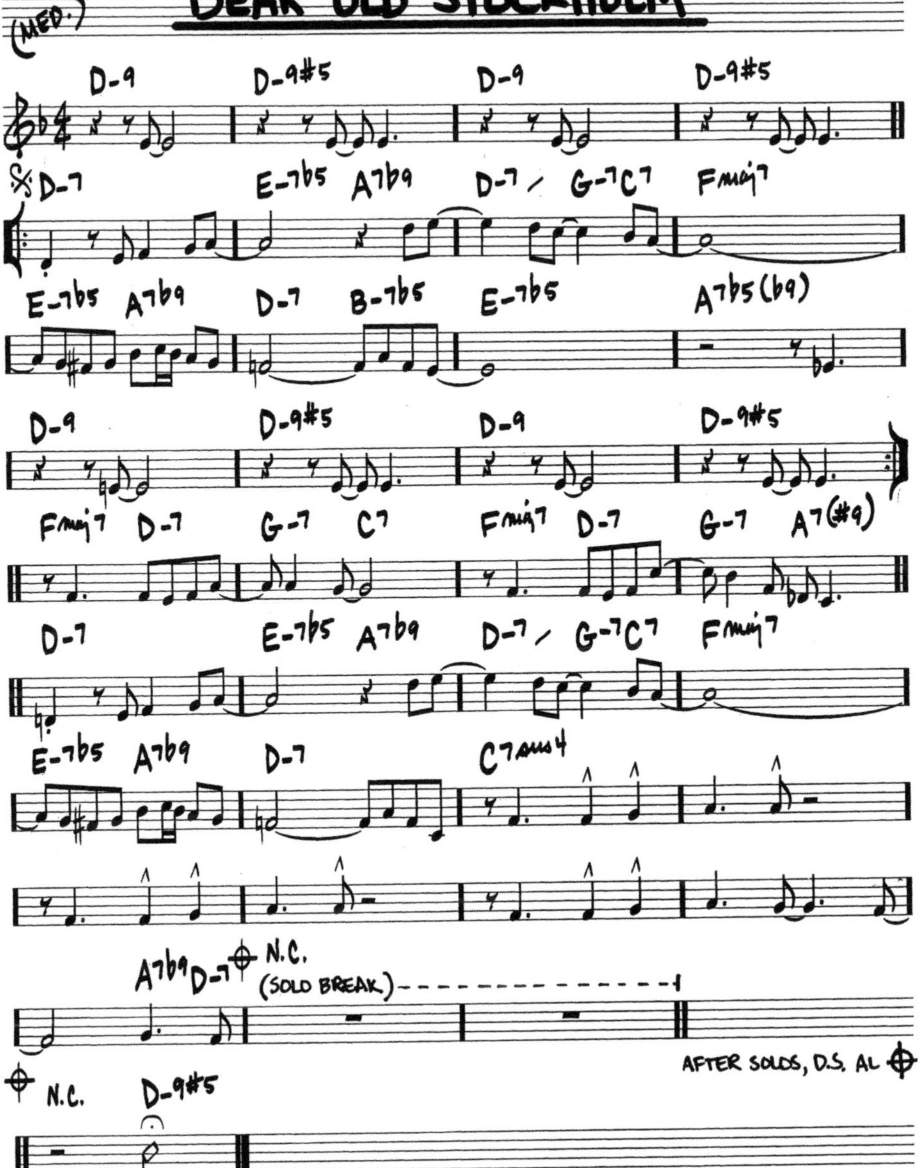

Copyright © 2004 by HAL LEONARD CORPORATION

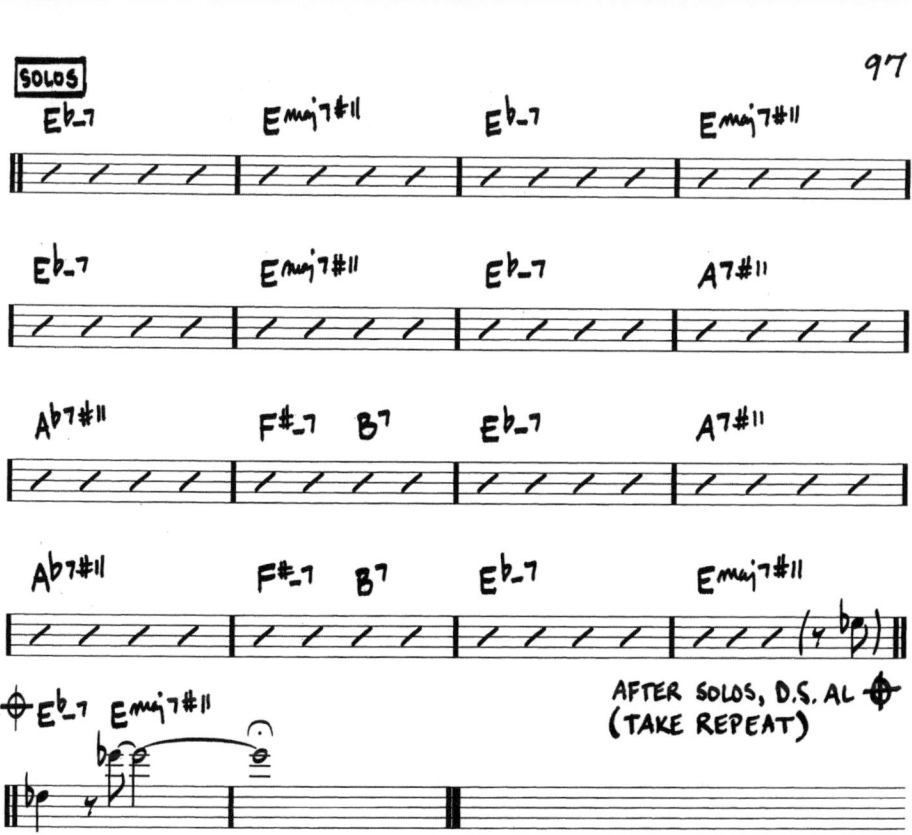

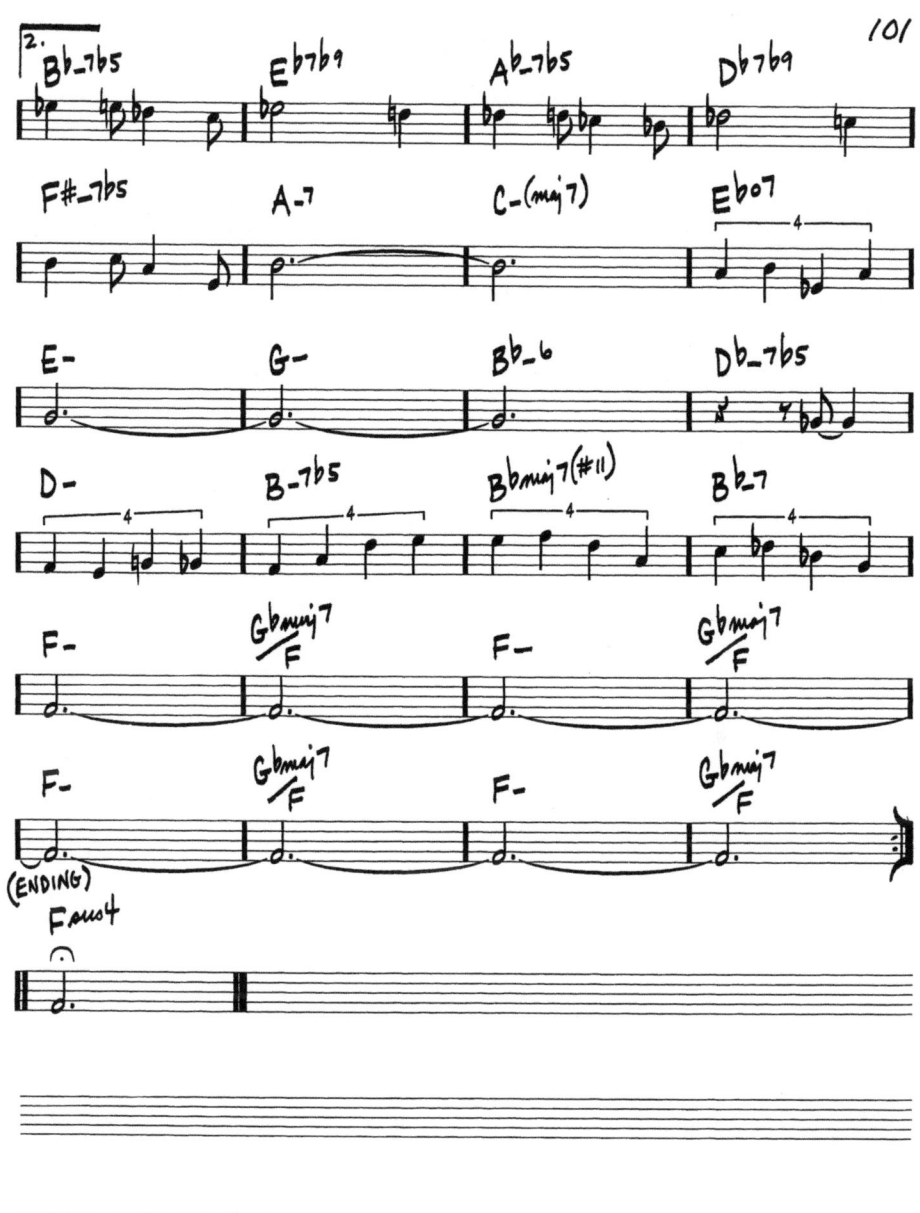

DOLORES

—WAYNE SHORTER

(FAST SWING)

Copyright © 1967 MIYAKO MUSIC
Copyright Renewed
All Rights Administered by IRVING MUSIC, INC.

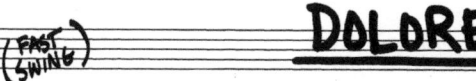

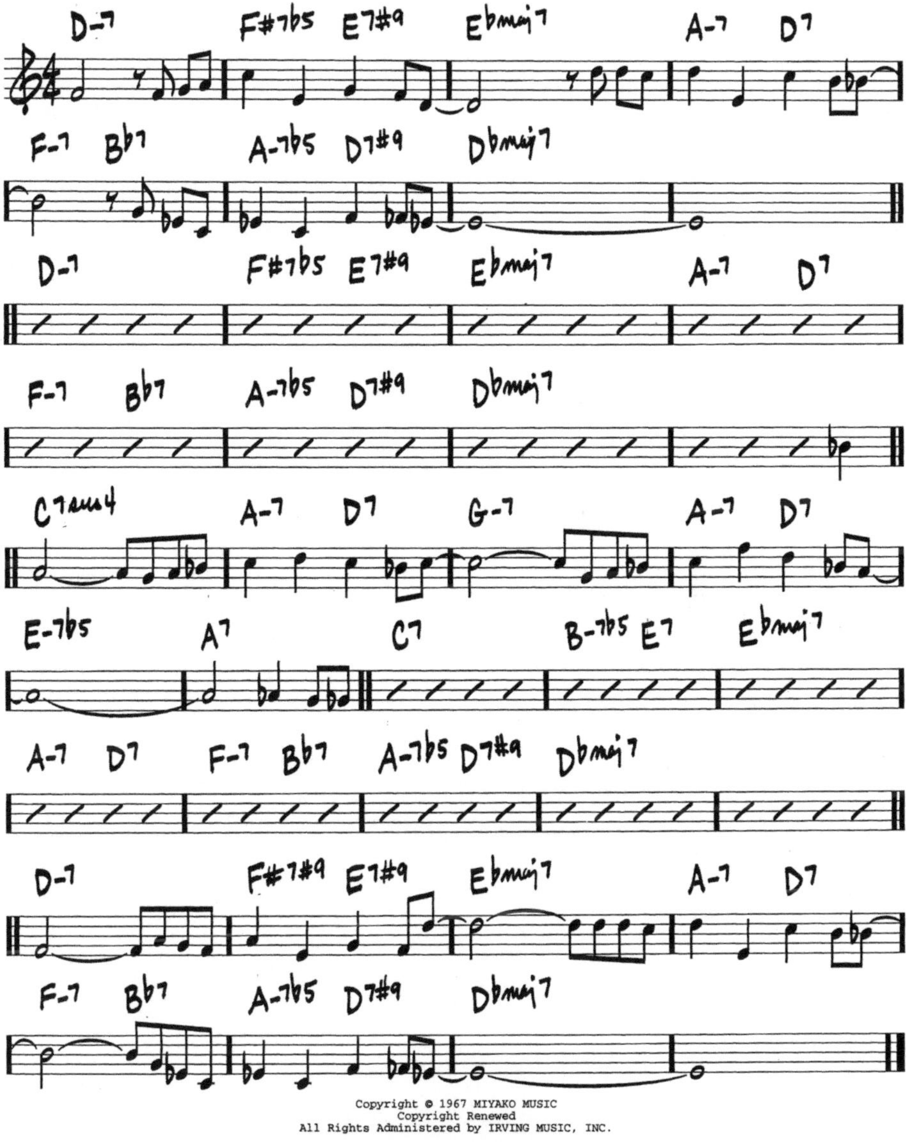

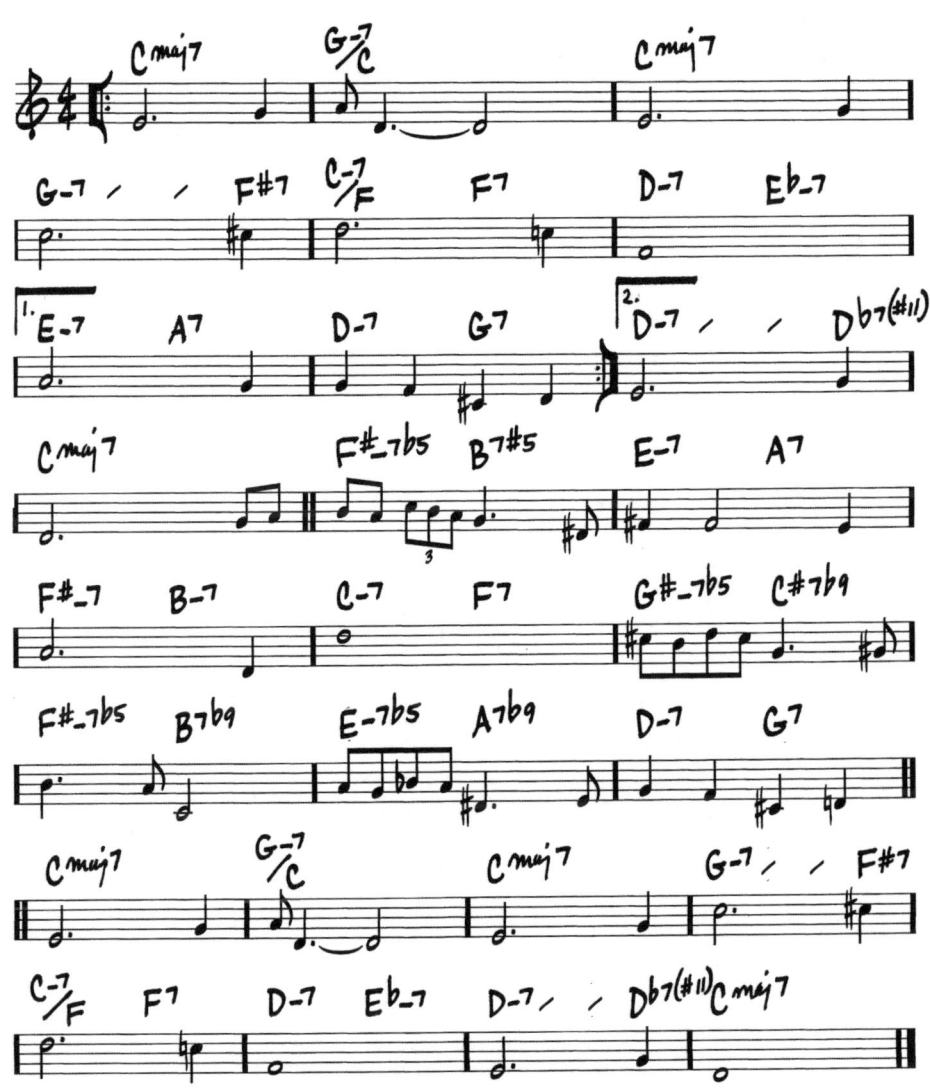

(MED. BALLAD)

EASY LIVING

—LEO ROBIN/RALPH RAINGER

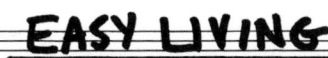

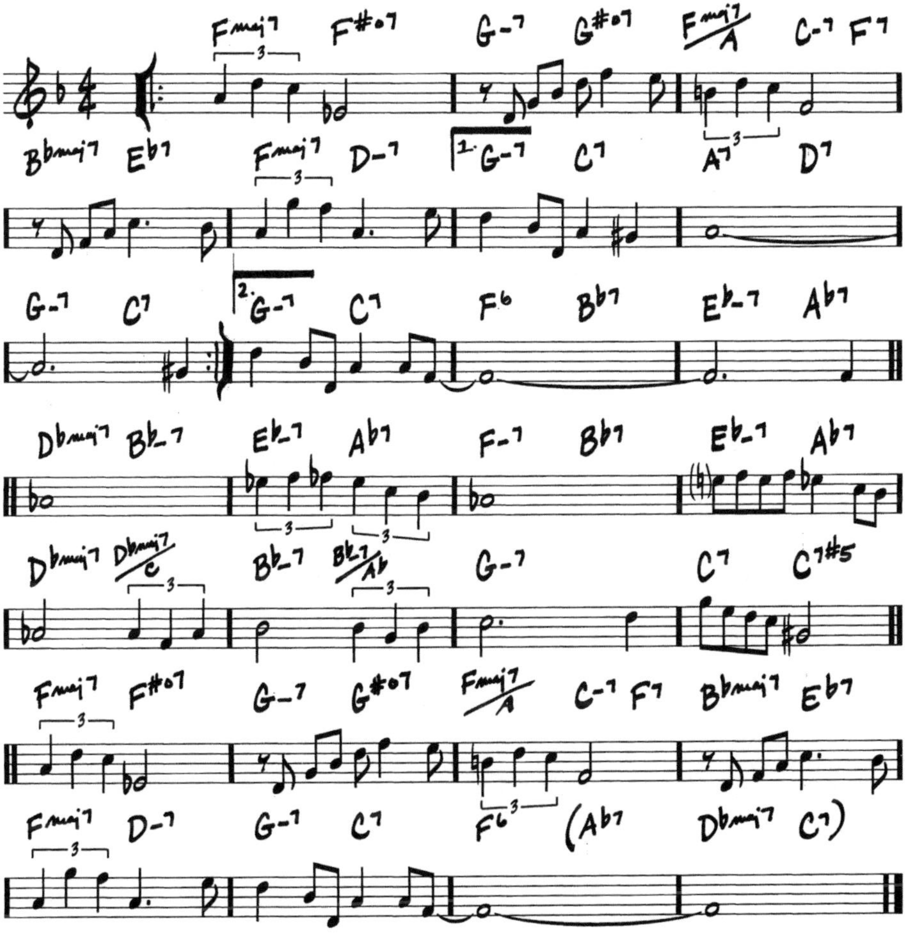

Copyright © 1937 (Renewed 1964) by Famous Music Corporation

E.S.P.

—WAYNE SHORTER

(FAST SWING)

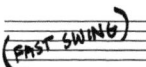

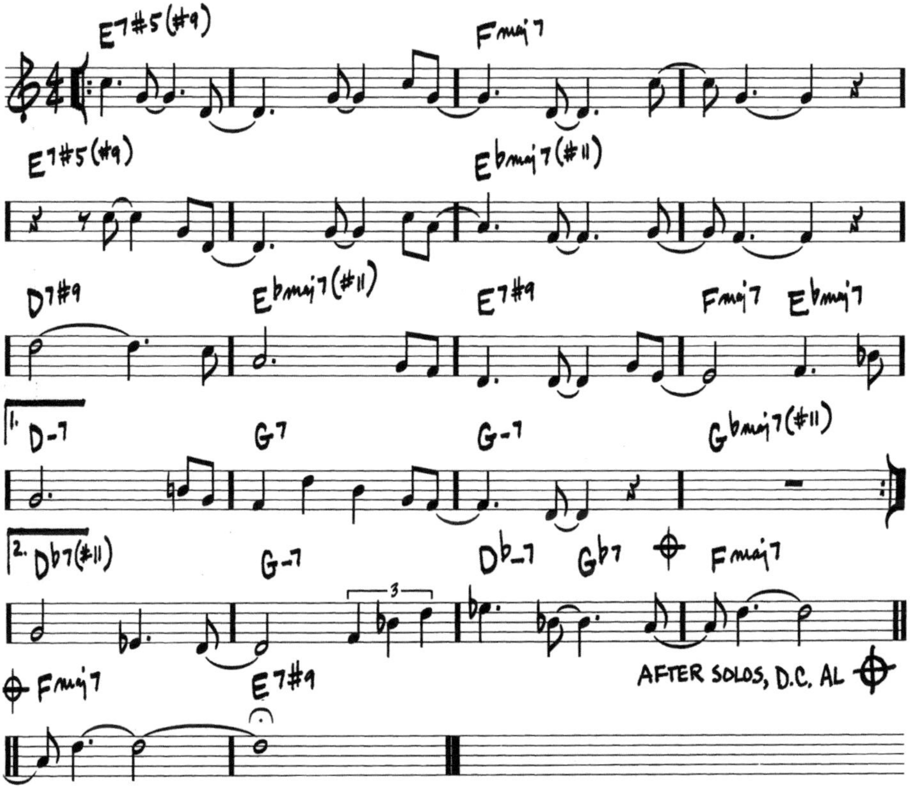

Copyright © 1965 MIYAKO MUSIC
Copyright Renewed
All Rights Administered by IRVING MUSIC, INC.

(MED. BALLAD)

A FINE ROMANCE

—JEROME KERN/
DOROTHY FIELDS

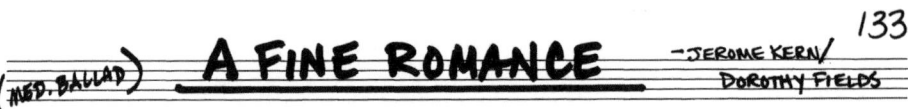

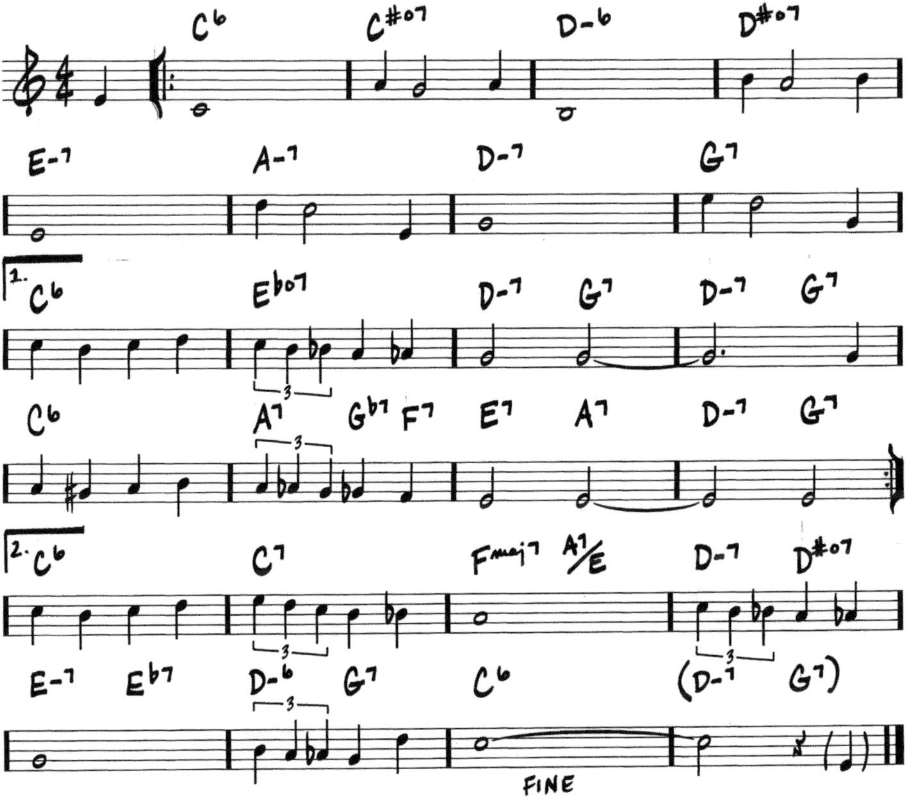

Copyright © 1936 UNIVERSAL - POLYGRAM INTERNATIONAL PUBLISHING, INC. and ALDI MUSIC
Copyright Renewed
All Rights for ALDI MUSIC Administered by THE SONGWRITERS GUILD OF AMERICA

500 MILES HIGH

(MED. LATIN)

– CHICK COREA/
NEVILLE POTTER

Copyright © 1978 UNIVERSAL MUSIC CORP.

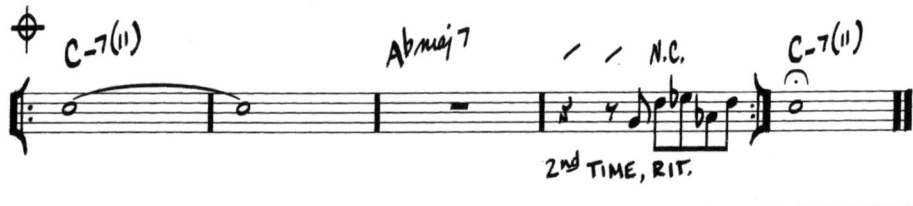

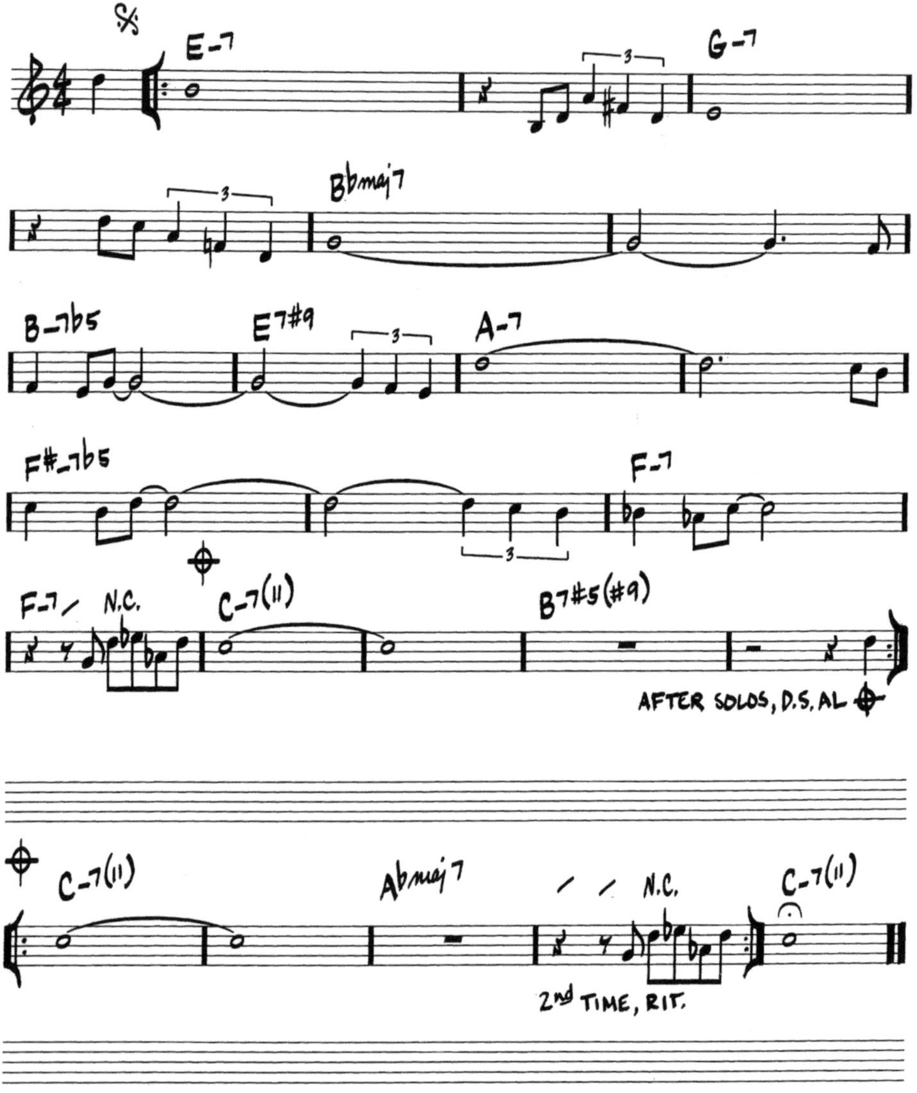

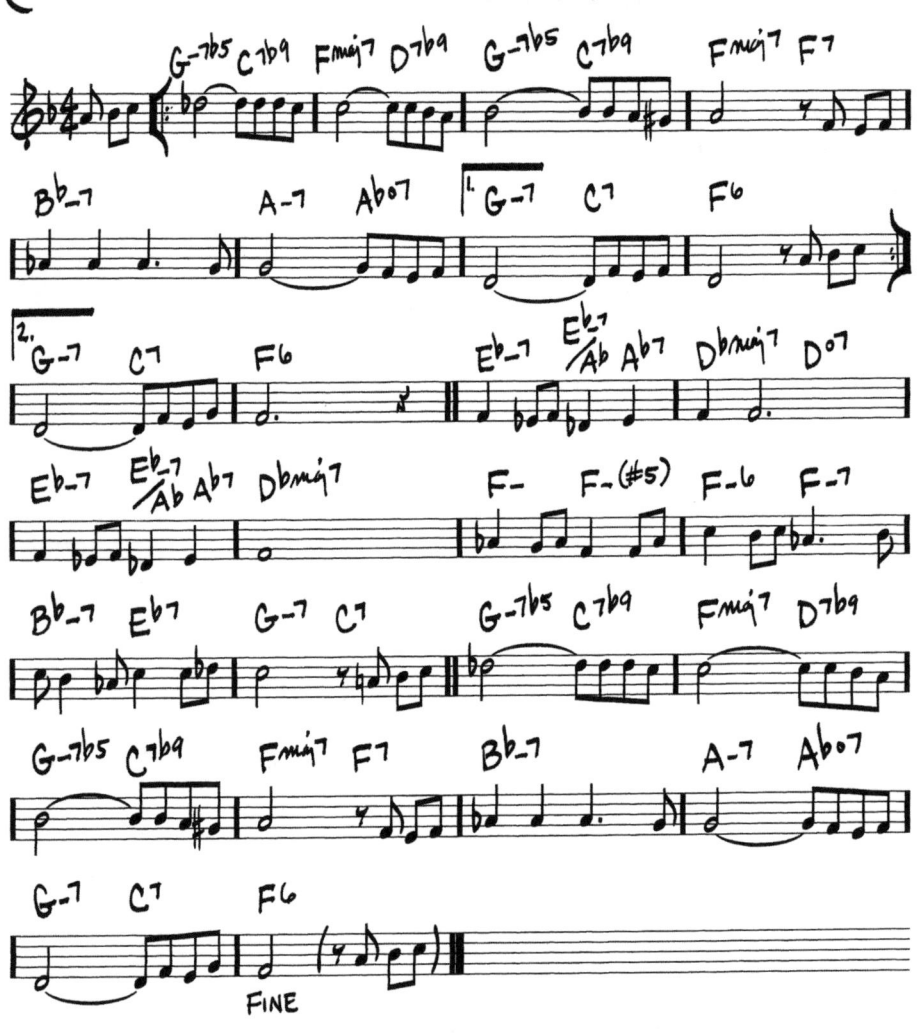

FREEDOM JAZZ DANCE — Eddie Harris

(Med. Funk-Rock)

REPEAT HEAD IN/OUT
OPEN SOLOS OVER Bb7

Full House

— John L. (Wes) Montgomery

(Jazz Waltz)

GEMINI

(FAST 3)

—JIMMY HEATH

Copyright © 1962 (Renewed 1990) by MJQ Music, Inc.

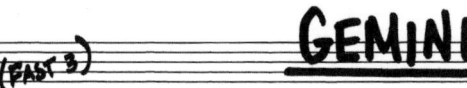

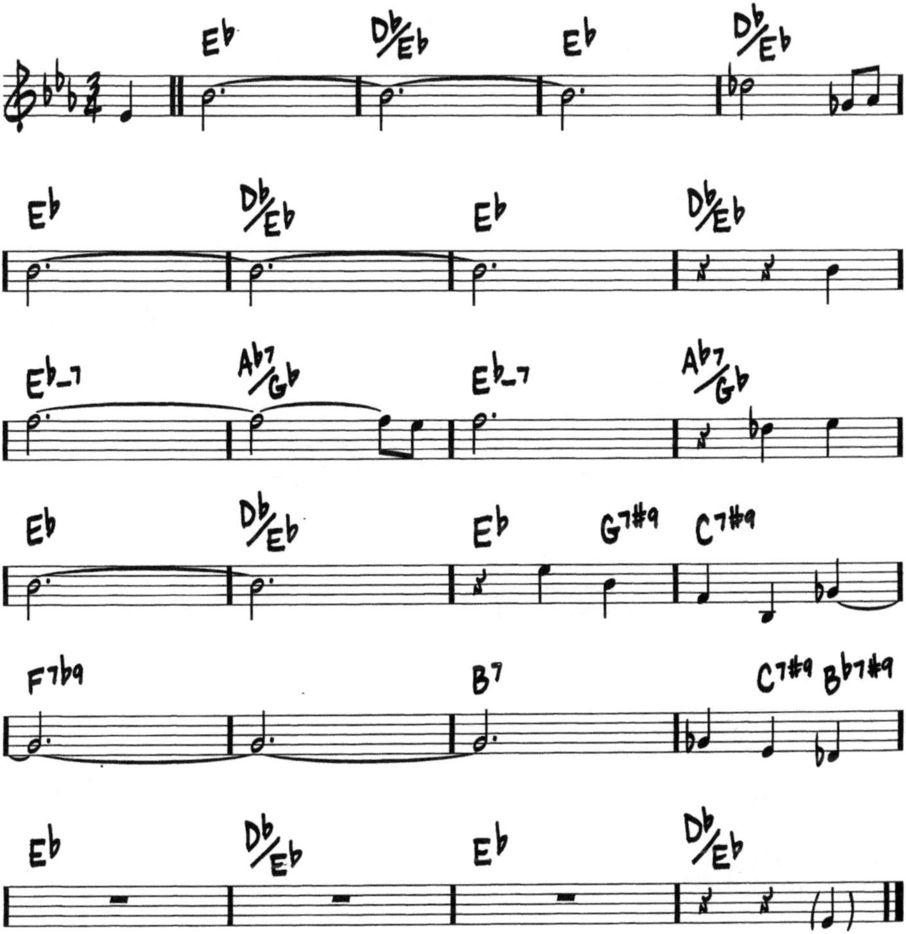

Get Happy

— Harold Arlen / Ted Koehler

152 (UP)

© 1929 WARNER BROS. INC. and S.A. MUSIC CO. (Renewed)

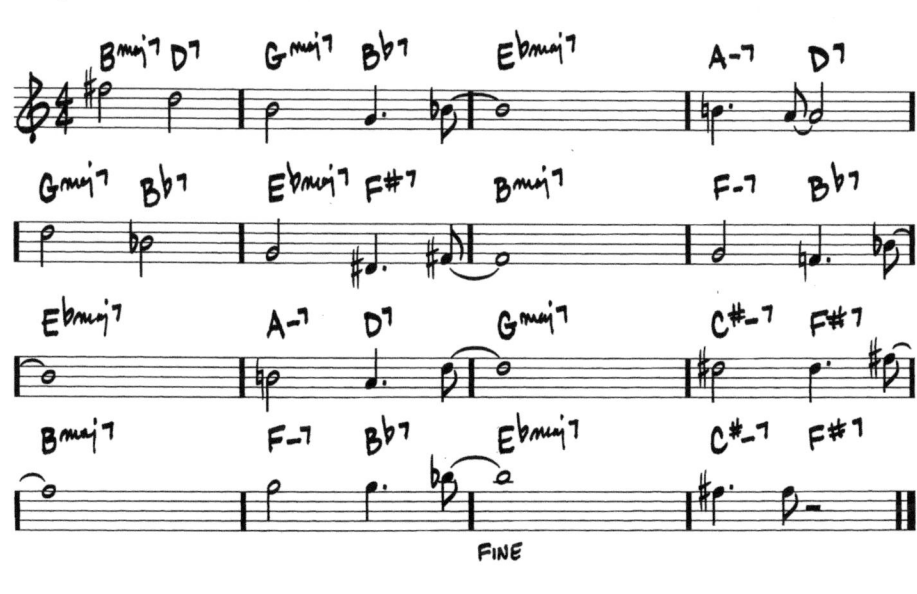

Gloria's Step

—Scott LeFaro

(Med. Swing)

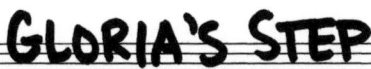

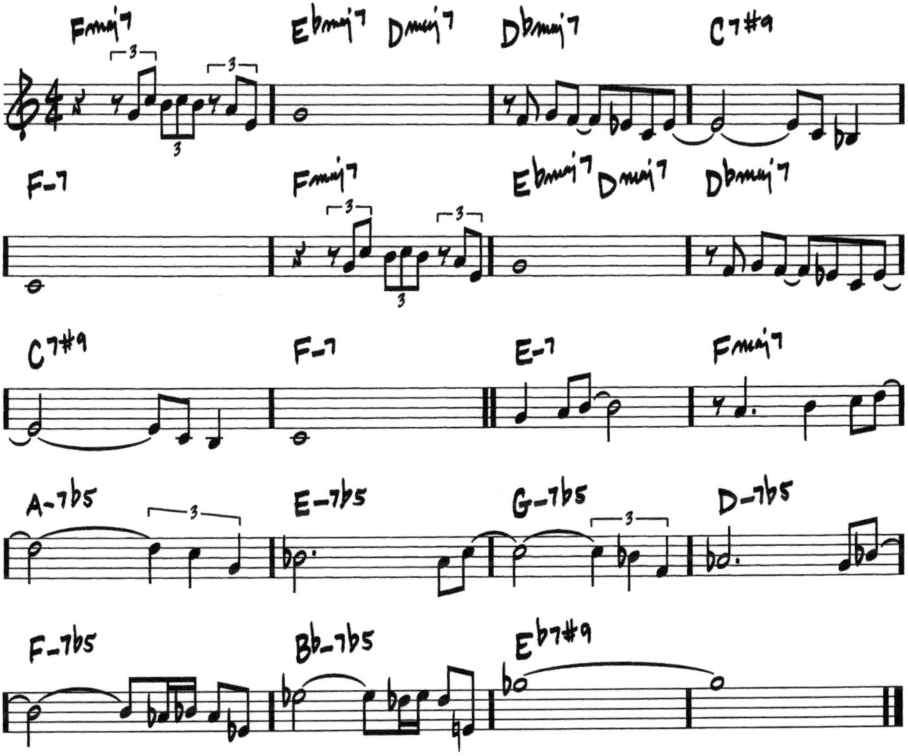

Copyright © 1962 Orpheum Music
Copyright Renewed

Good Morning Heartache

(Ballad) — Dan Fisher / Irene Higginbotham / Ervin Drake

GRAND CENTRAL

—JOHN COLTRANE

(♩ UP = 258)

Copyright © 1977 JOWCOL MUSIC

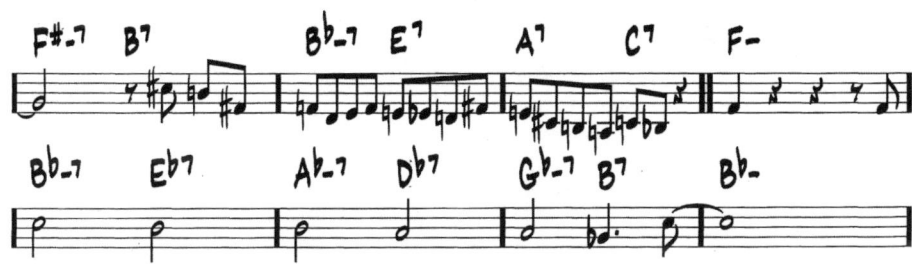

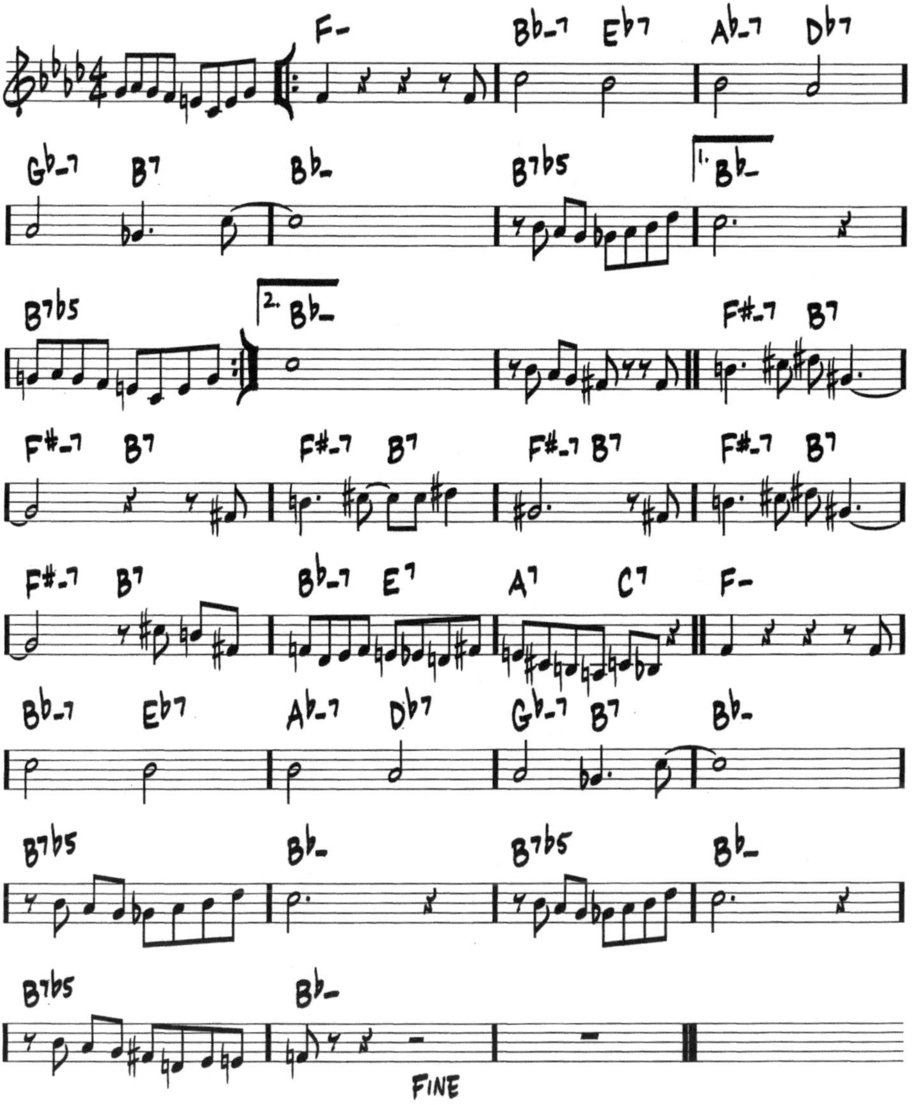

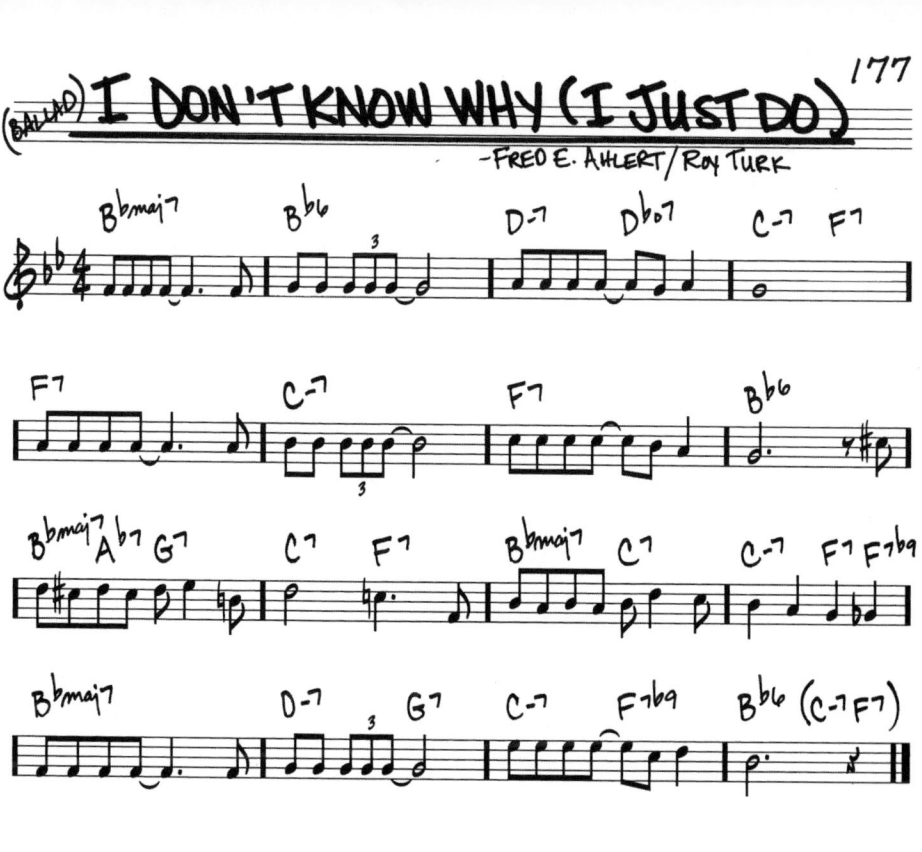

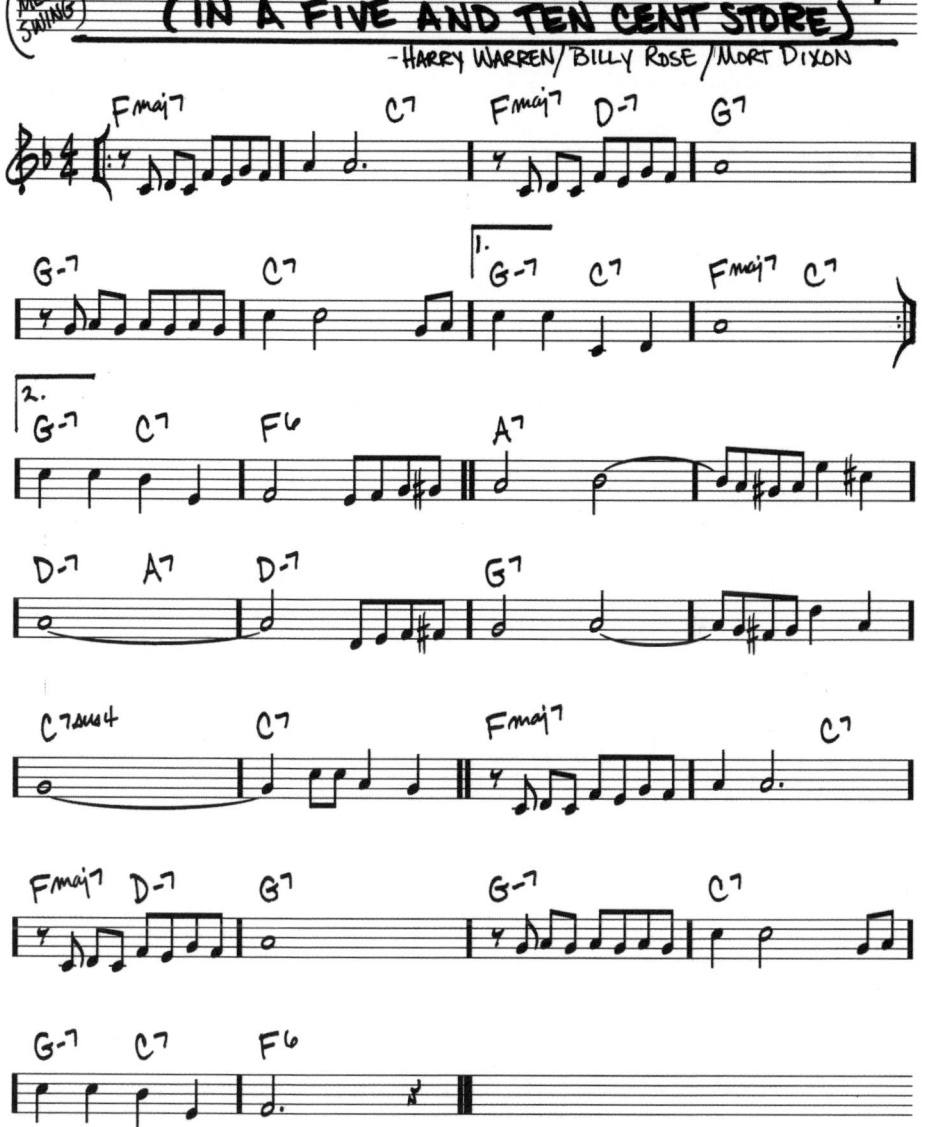

I'll Get By (As Long As I Have You)

(Med. Swing)

— Fred E. Ahlert / Roy Turk

I'll Remember April

— Pat Johnson / Don Raye / Gene De Paul

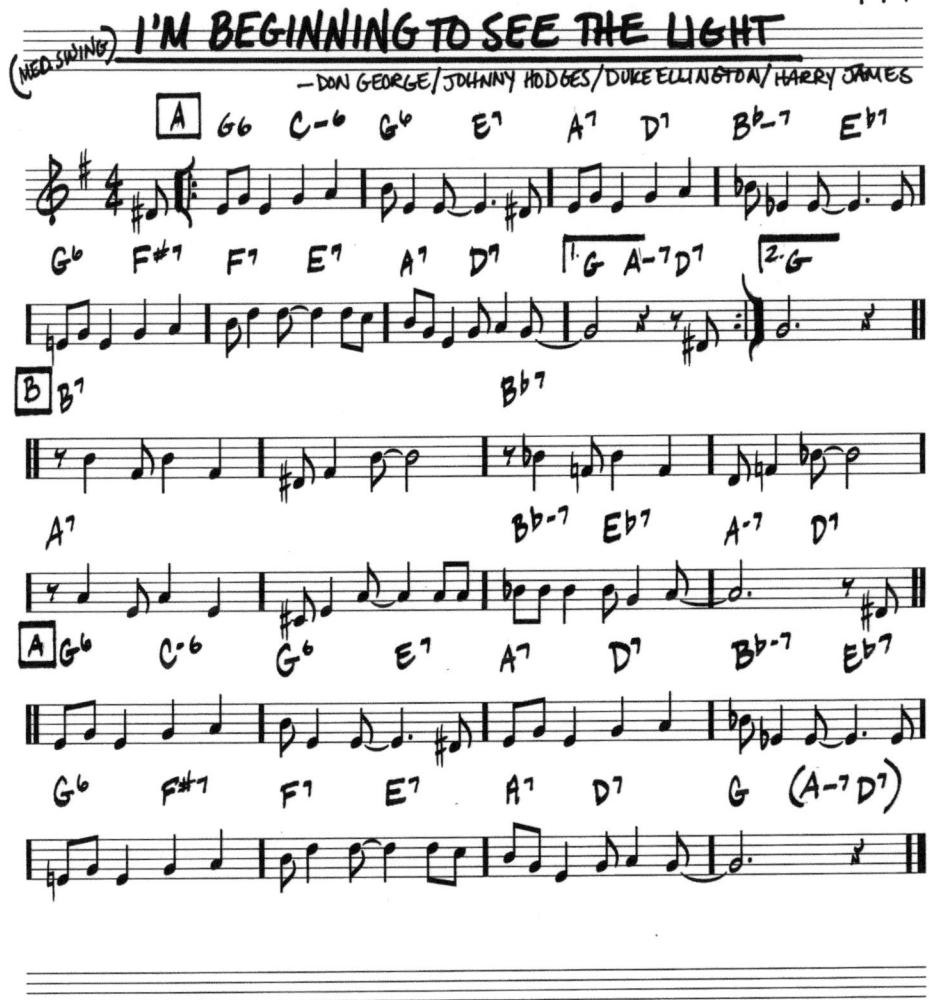

I'VE NEVER BEEN IN LOVE BEFORE
(Ballad)
— FRANK LOESSER

IMPRESSIONS
— John Coltrane

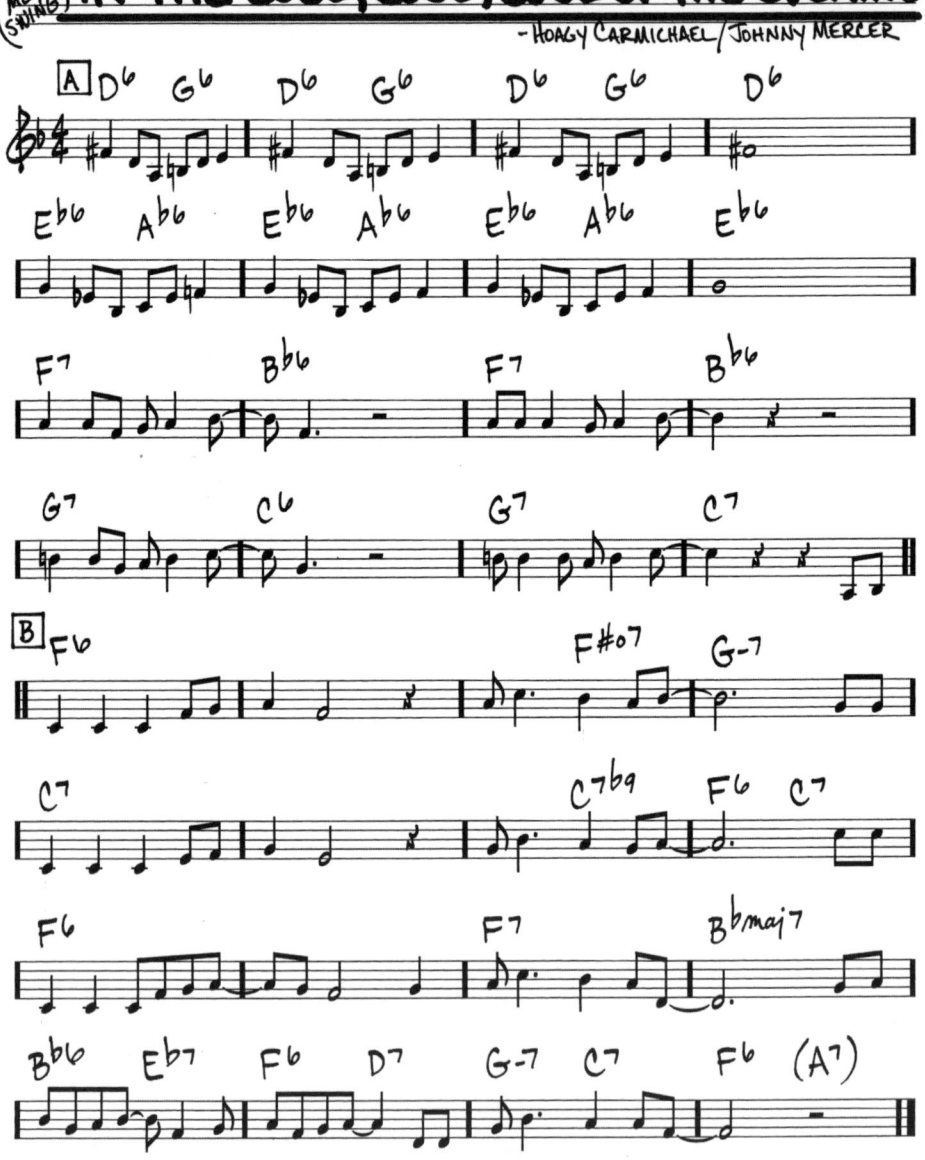

Is You Is, Or Is You Ain't (Ma' Baby)

– Billy Austin / Louis Jordan

ISRAEL

(SWING)

—JOHN CARISI

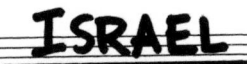

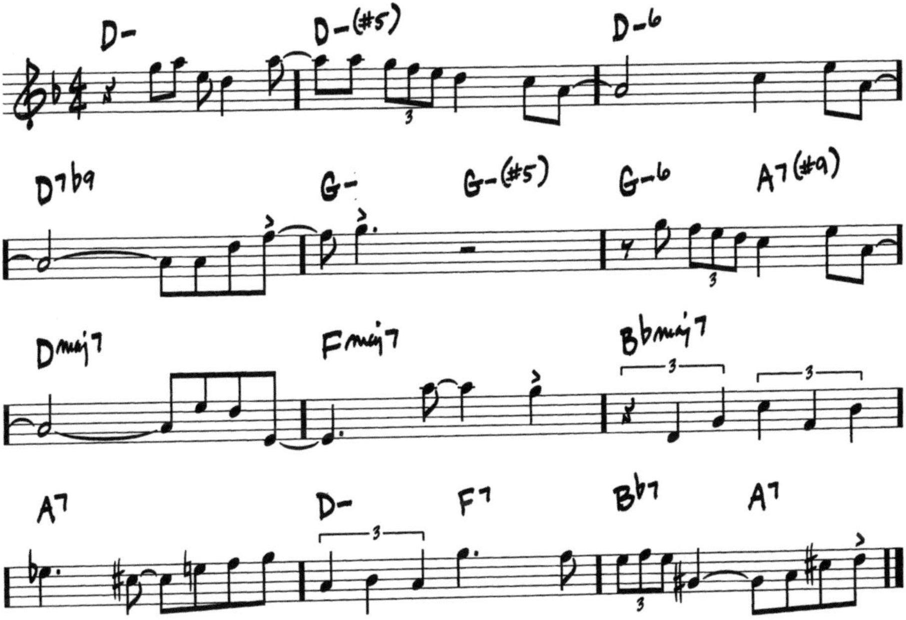

© 1954 (Renewed 1982) BEECHWOOD MUSIC CORP.

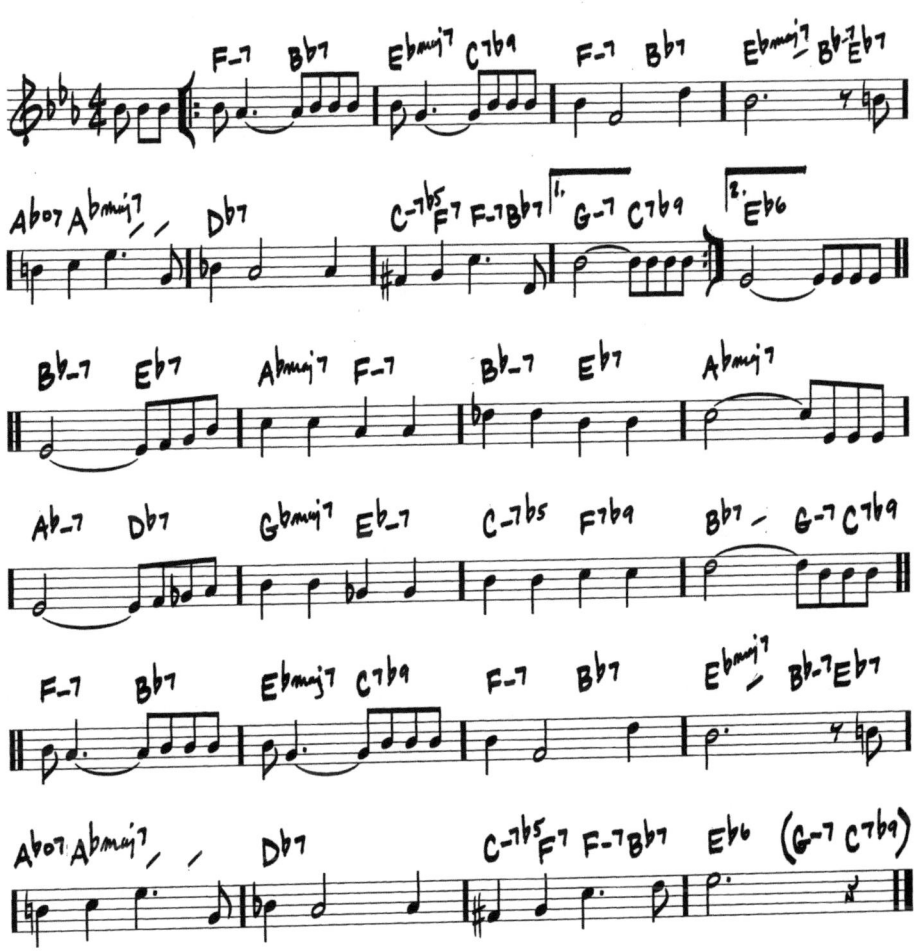

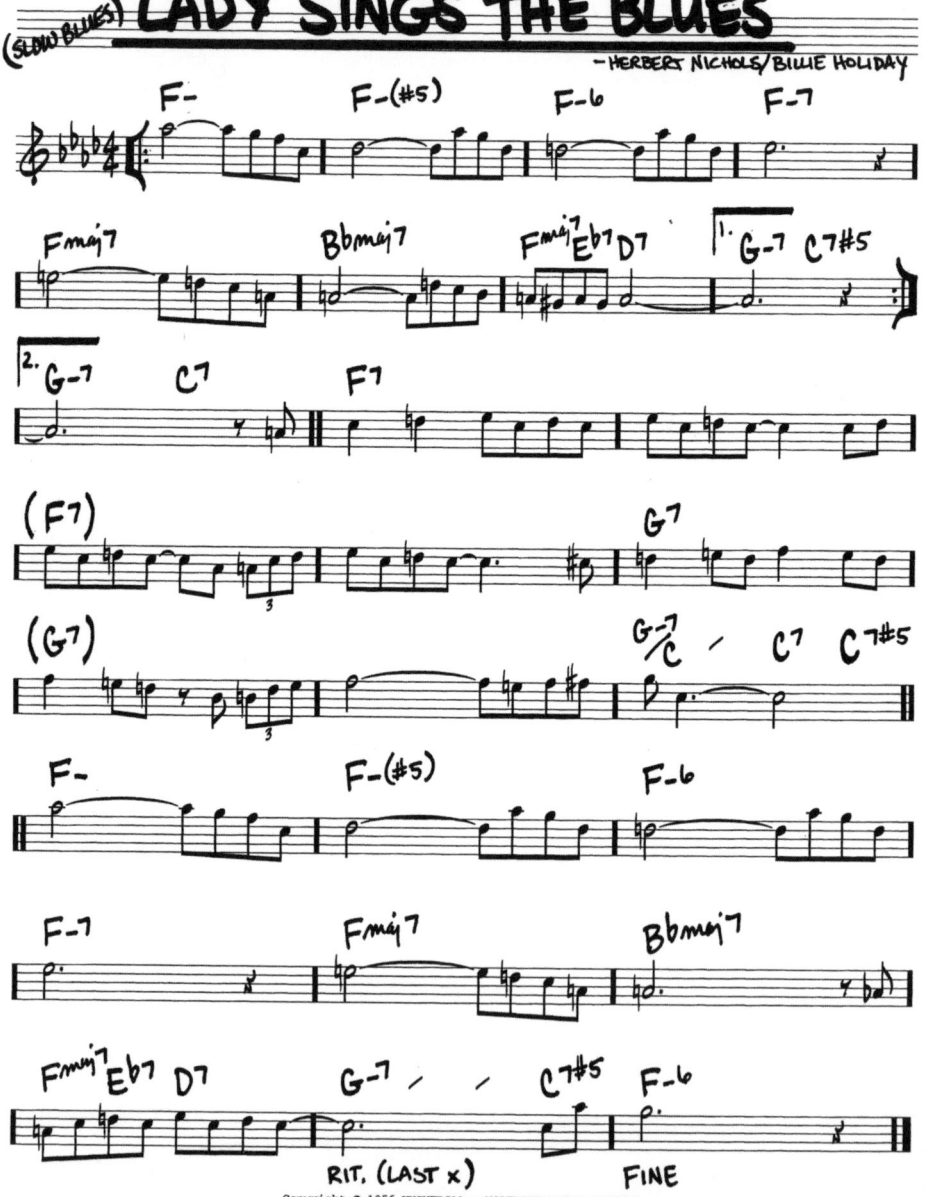

LAS VEGAS TANGO
— GIL EVANS

(EVEN 8ths)

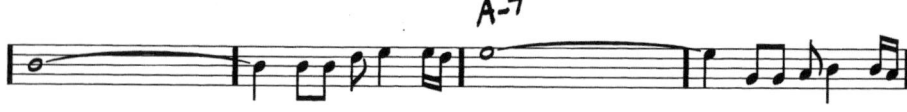

FINE

AFTER SOLOS, D.C. AL FINE
(TAKE REPEAT)

LAZY BIRD

-JOHN COLTRANE

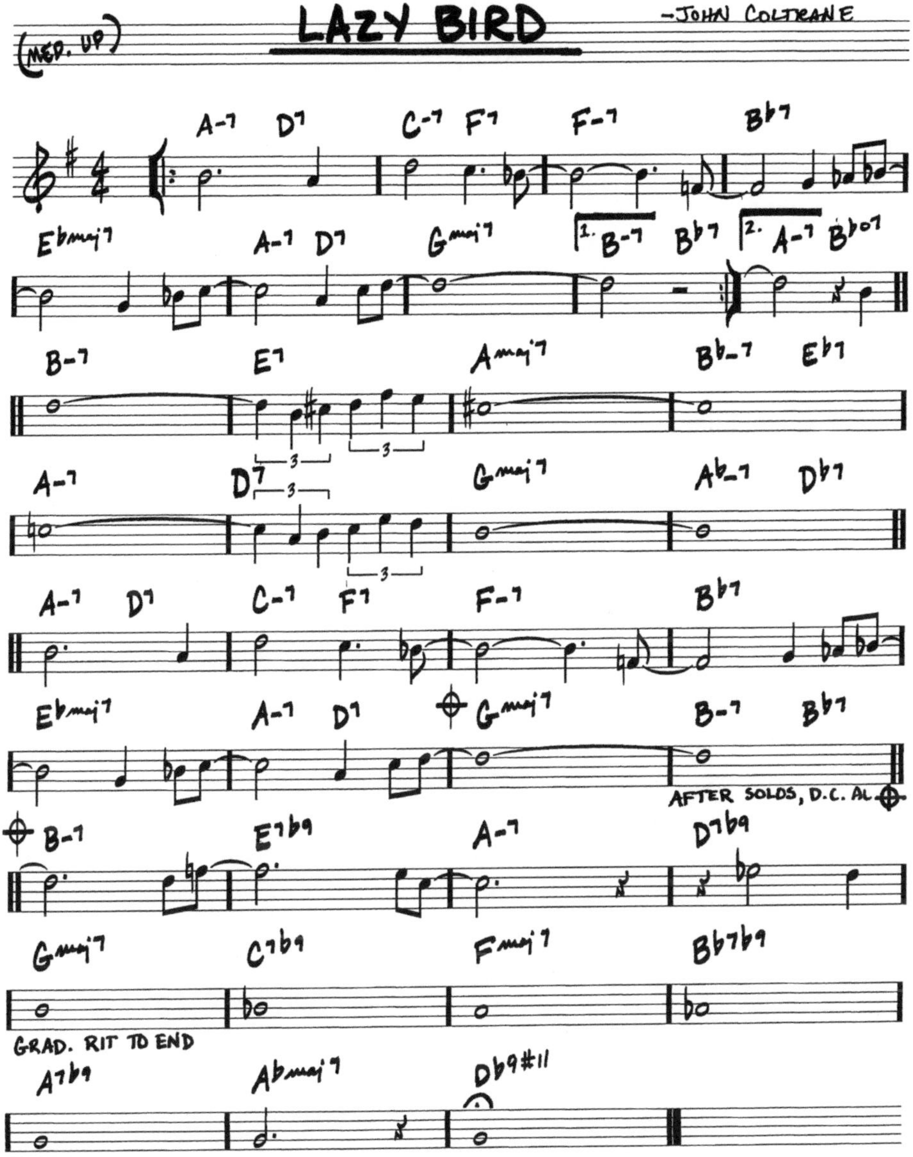

Copyright © 1957 (Renewed 1985) JOWCOL MUSIC

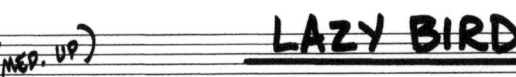

241
LET'S GET AWAY FROM IT ALL
(MED. SWING) — Tom Adair / Matt Dennis

Ab-7
Bbo7
Cbmaj7
Ebo7
D7
Db-7
B-7
A-7
(A-7)
AFTER SOLOS, D.C. AL
Ebo7
D7
Db-7
B-7
A-7
G-7

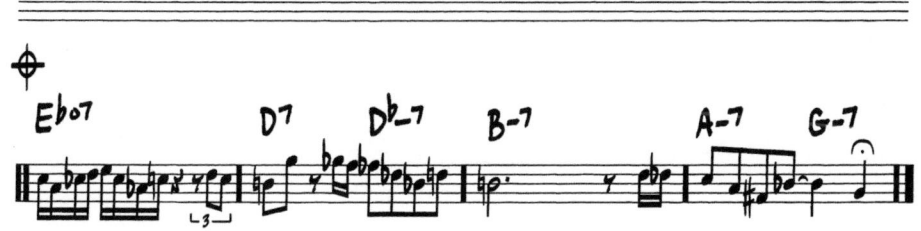

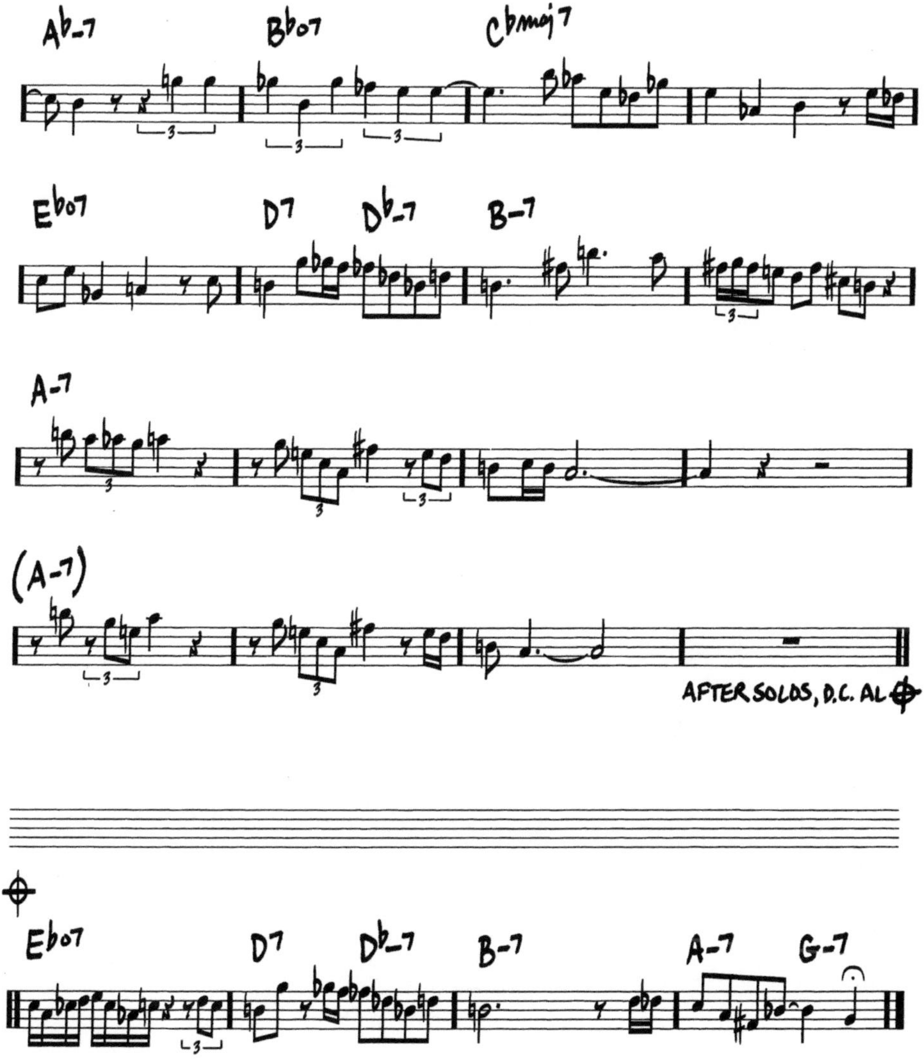

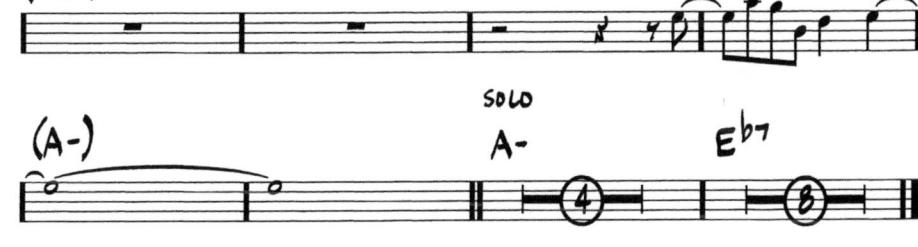

LITTLE WALTZ
— Ron Carter

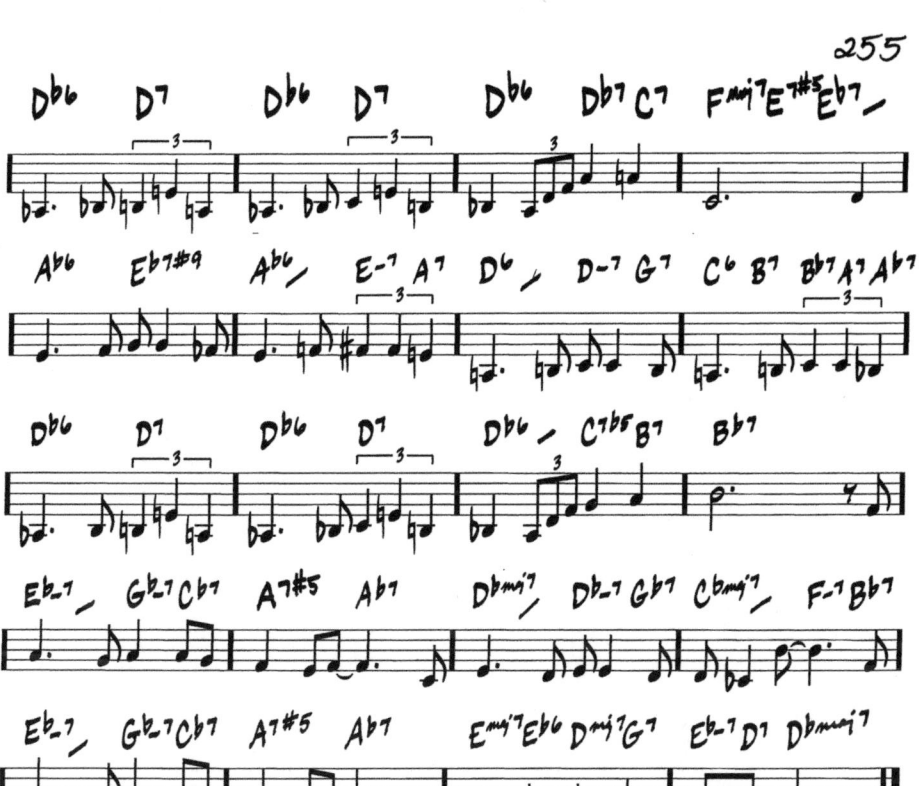

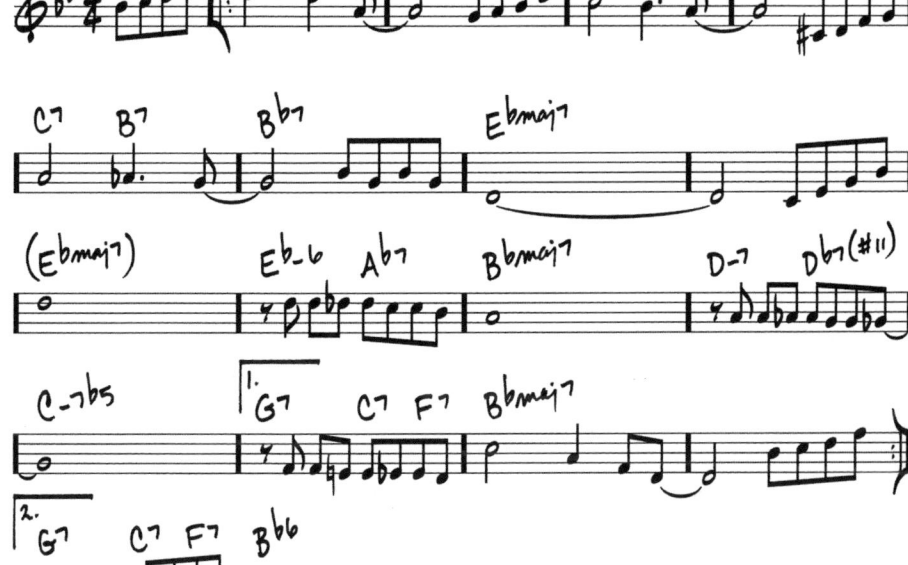

MILANO

(MED. SLOW)

JOHN LEWIS

Copyright © 1955 (Renewed 1983) by MJQ Music, Inc.

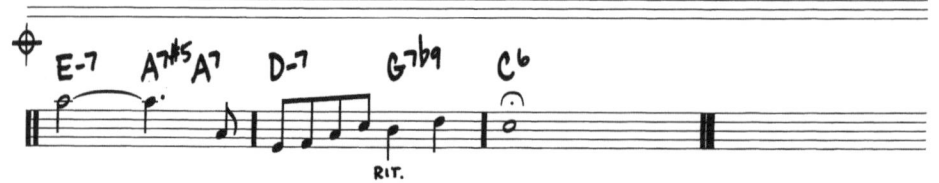

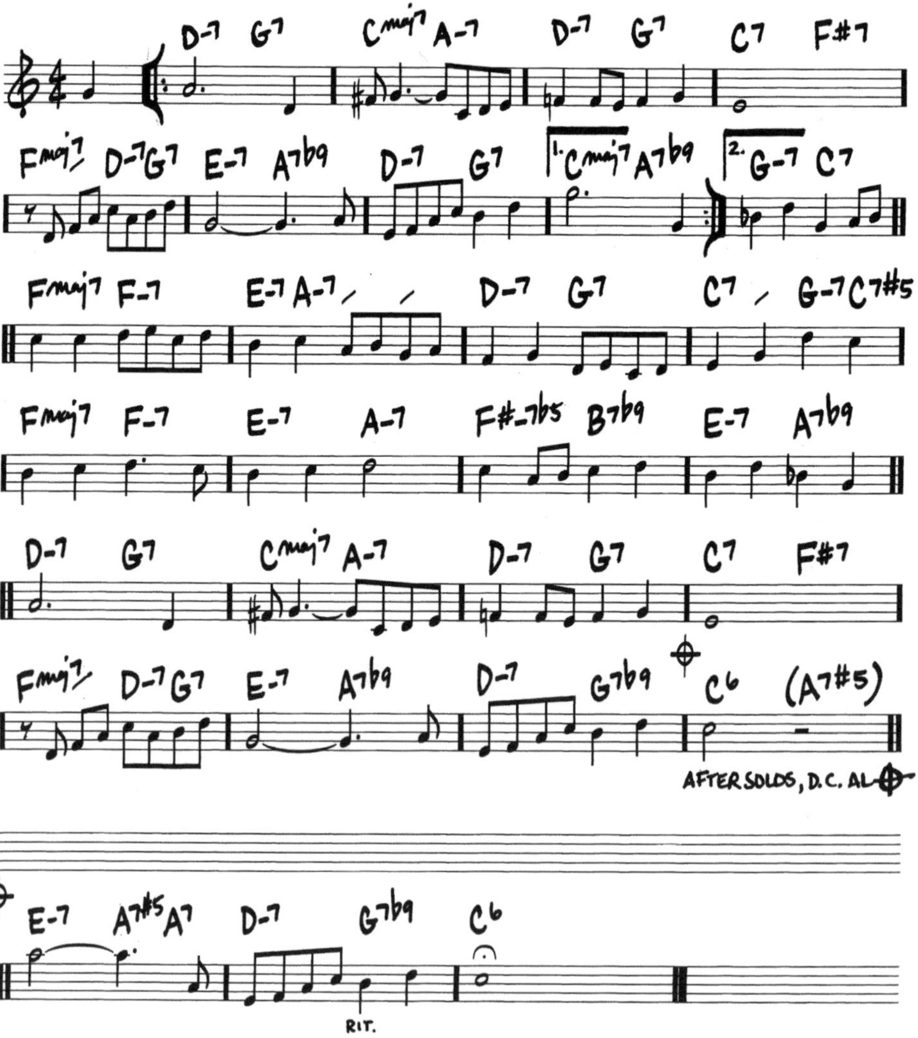

MISTY

(BALLAD)

–ERROLL GARNER

Copyright © 1954 by Octave Music Publishing Corporation
Copyright Renewed 1982

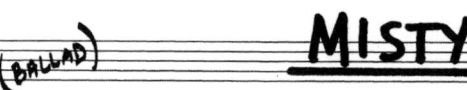

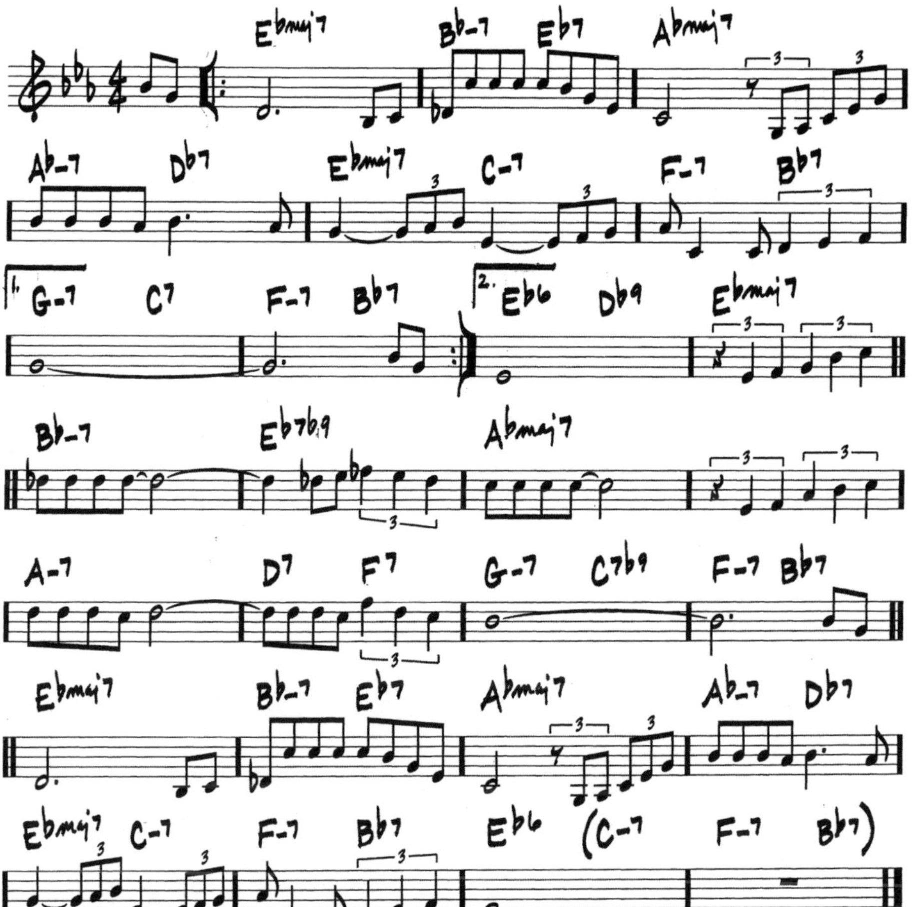

MONA LISA

(BALLAD)

-JAY LIVINGSTON/
RAY EVANS

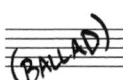

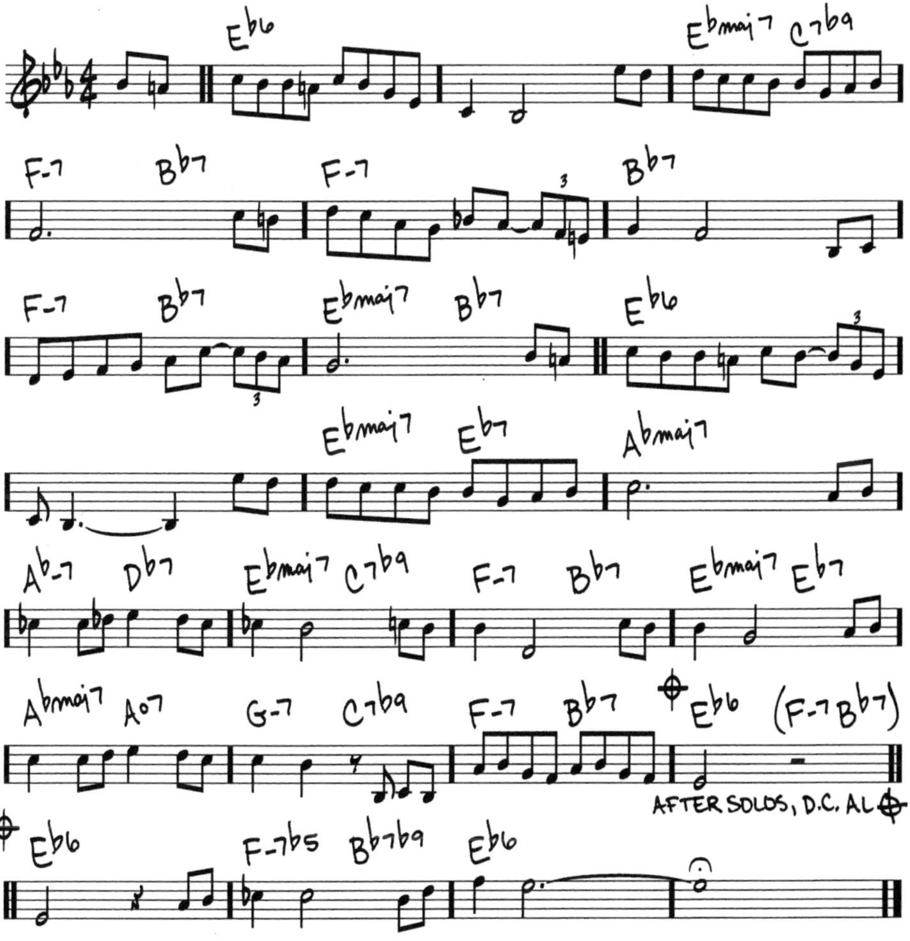

Copyright © 1949 (Renewed 1976) by Famous Music Corporation

LAST TIME, TO OPEN SOLOS IN 4/4 ON F#-7
AFTER SOLOS, FADE W/ DRUMS

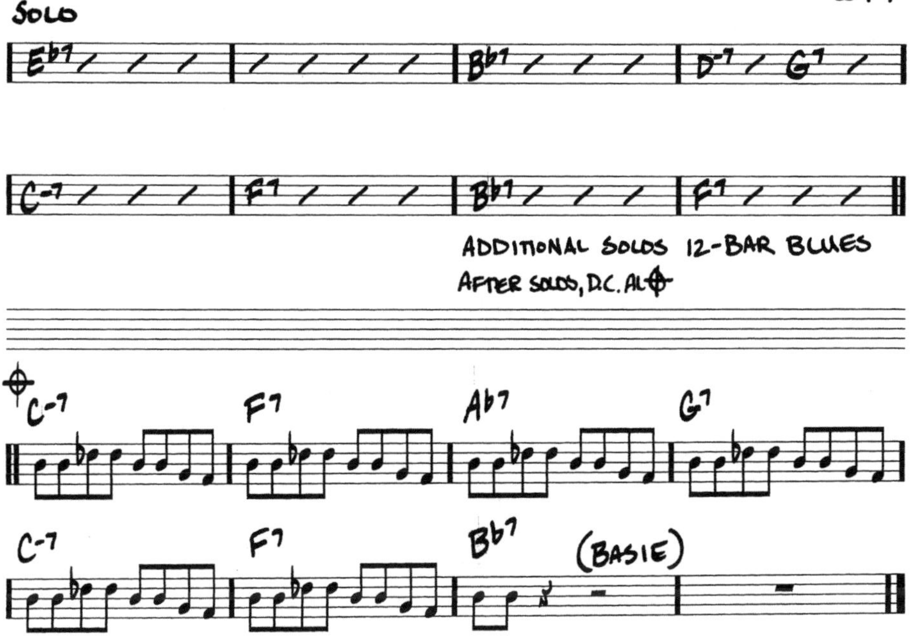

Solo

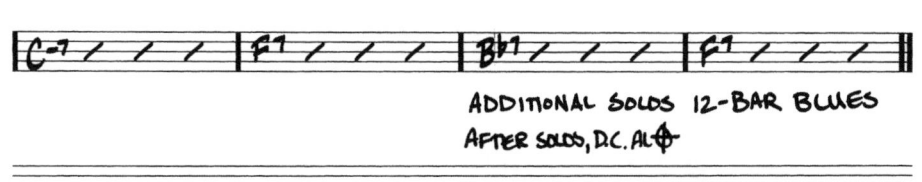

ADDITIONAL SOLOS 12-BAR BLUES
AFTER SOLOS, D.C. AL ⊕

NO MOON AT ALL

(MED. SWING)

– DAVE MANN / REDD EVANS

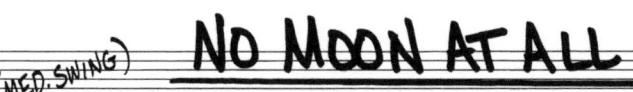

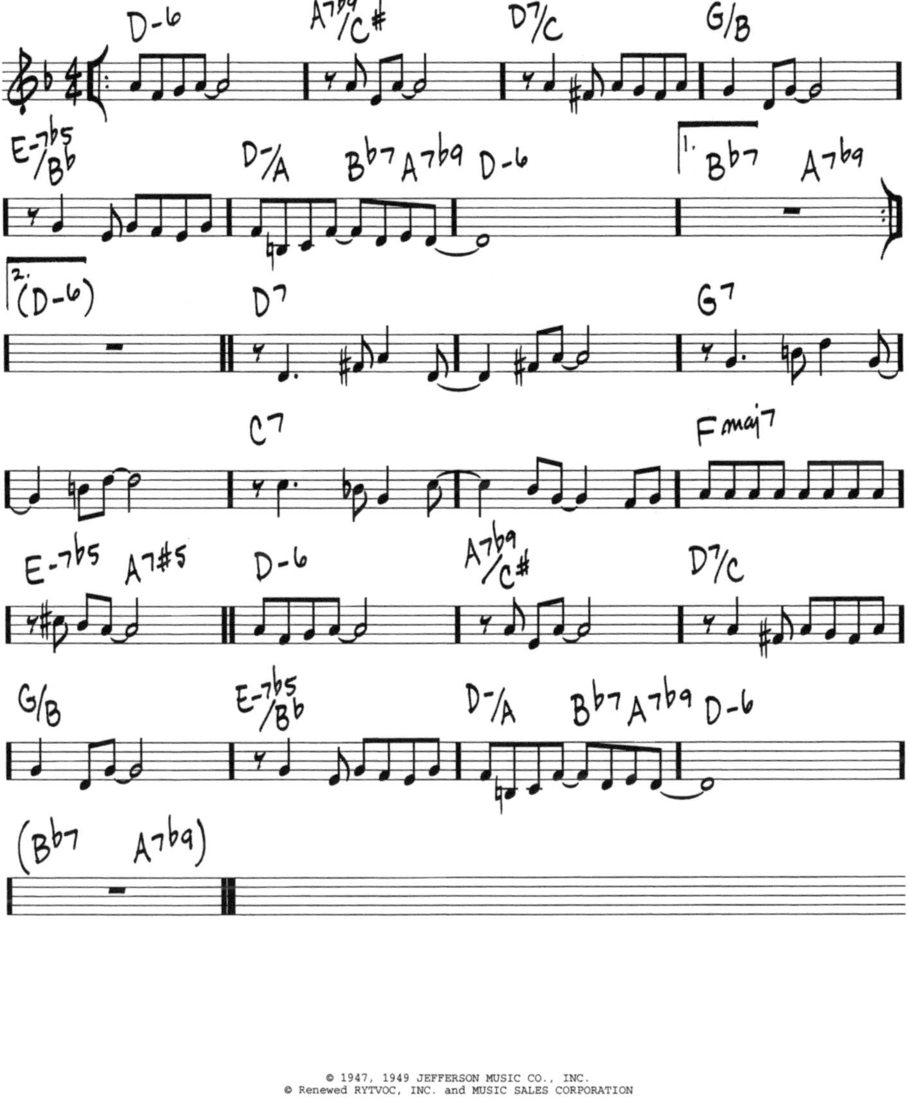

© 1947, 1949 JEFFERSON MUSIC CO., INC.
© Renewed RYTVOC, INC. and MUSIC SALES CORPORATION

ORBITS

—WAYNE SHORTER

(FAST SWING)

Copyright © 1967 MIYAKO MUSIC
Copyright Renewed
All Rights Administered by IRVING MUSIC, INC.

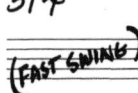

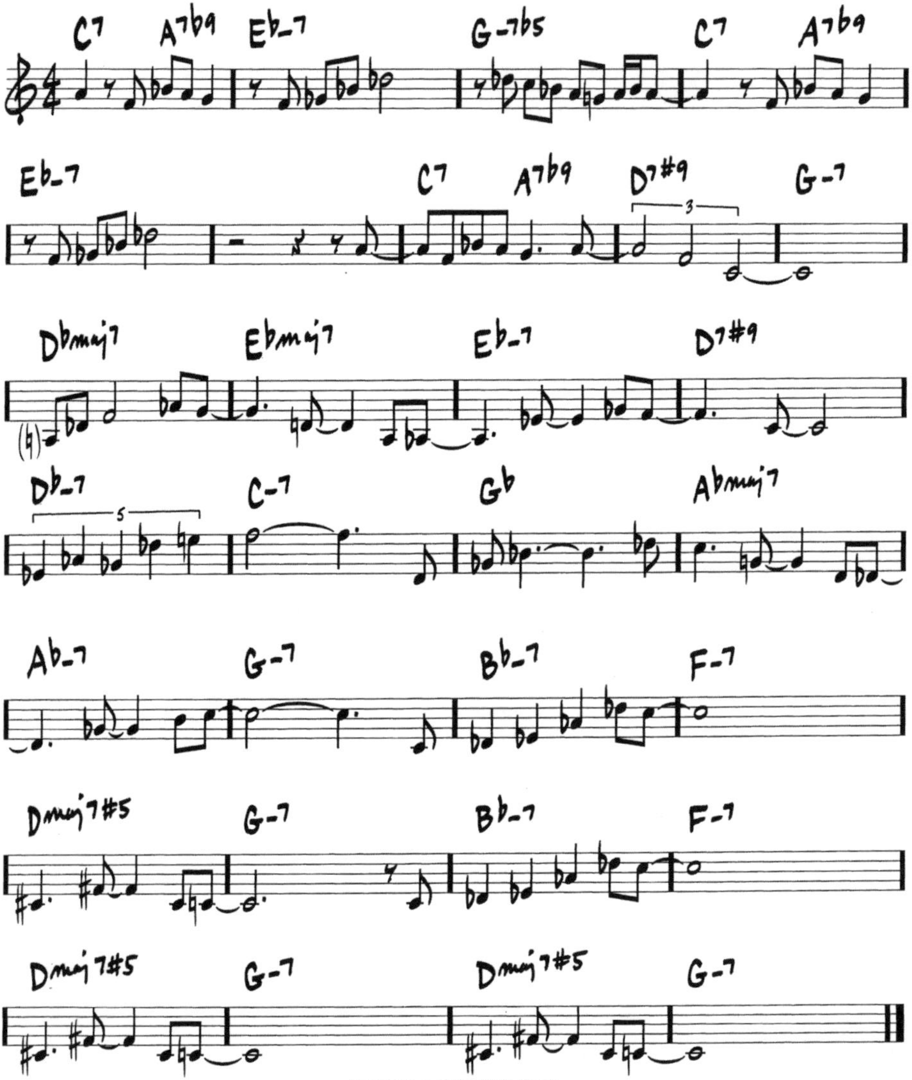

PAPER DOLL

(SLOW)

—JOHNNY S. BLACK

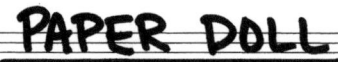

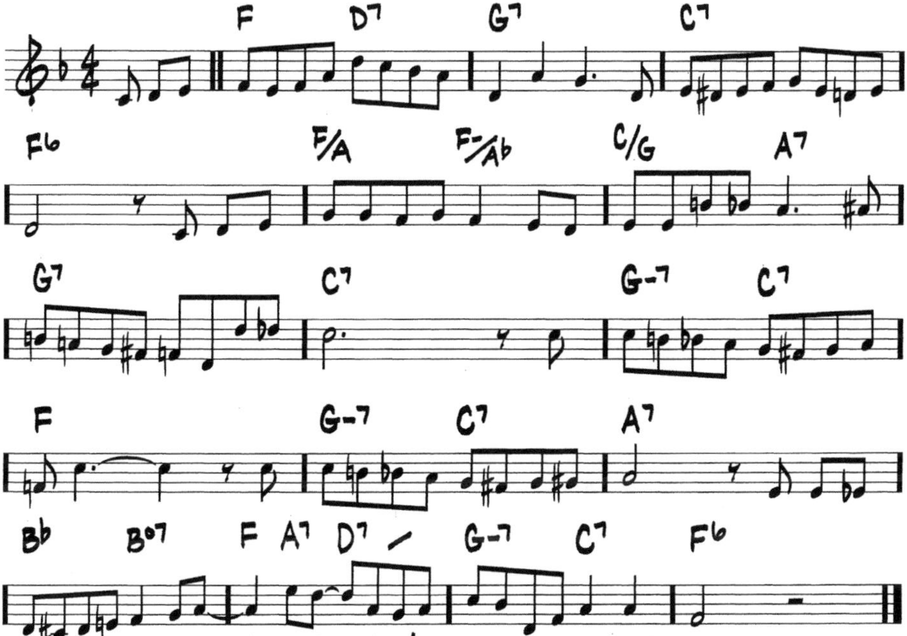

ALSO PLAYED ¢ SWING — DOUBLE RHYTHM VALUES
DRUMS IN DOUBLE TIME

Copyright © 2004 by HAL LEONARD CORPORATION

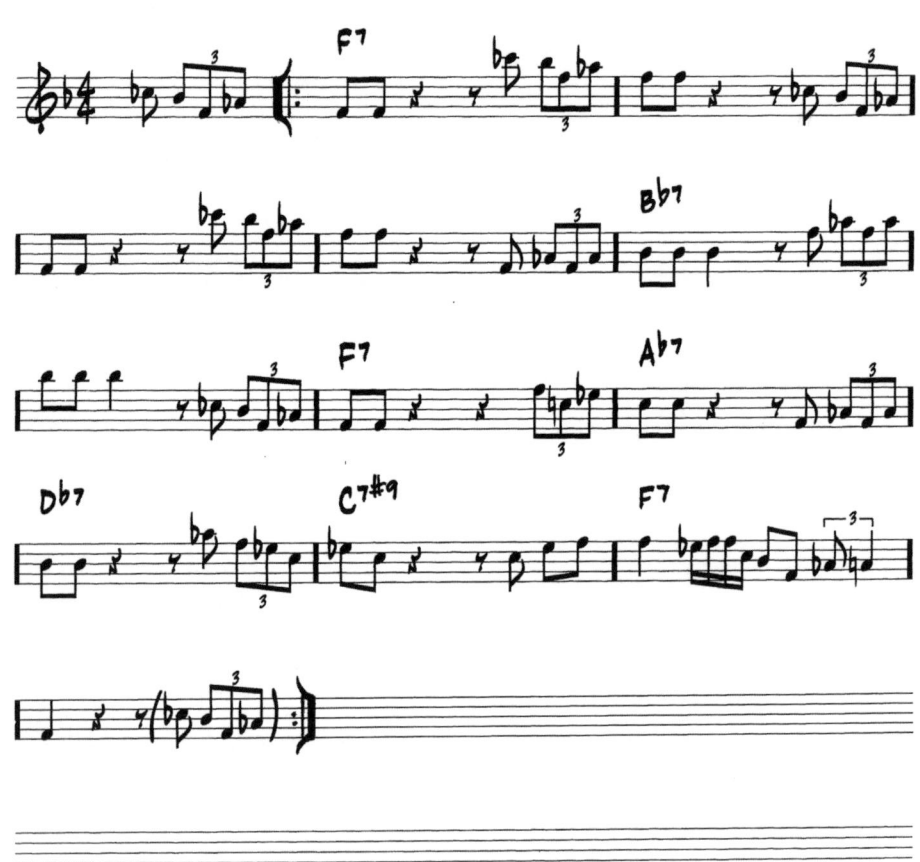

(UPTEMPO)

PRINCE OF DARKNESS

—WAYNE SHORTER

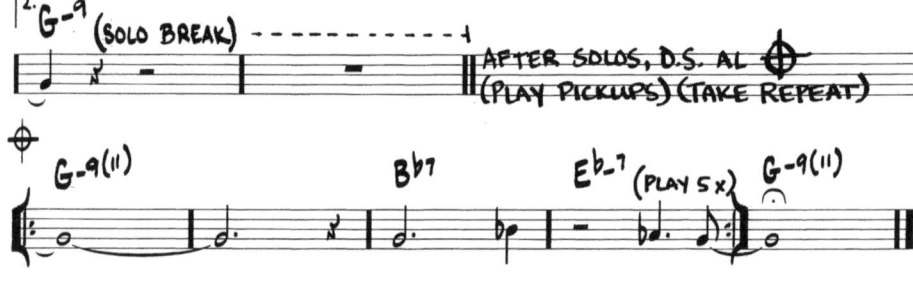

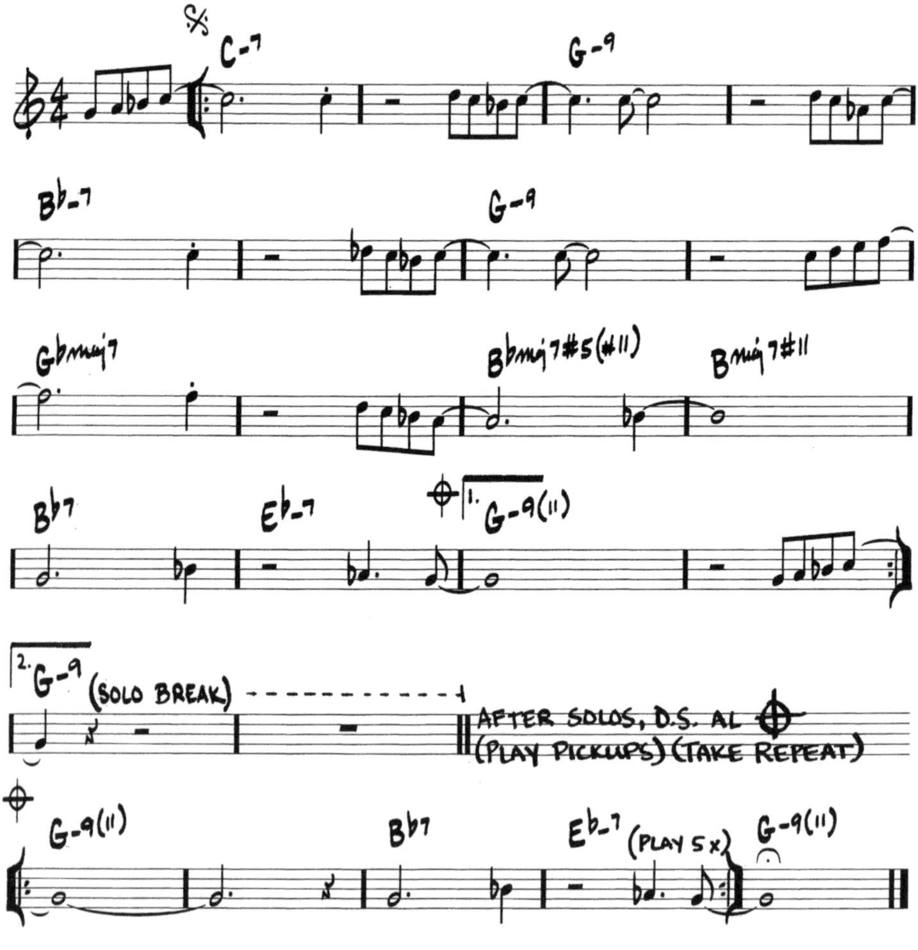

Copyright © 1968 MIYAKO MUSIC
Copyright Renewed
All Rights Administered by IRVING MUSIC, INC.

PUSSY CAT DUES

(SLOW SWING ♩=68)

- CHARLES MINGUS

For more than a snapshot version of Mingus, see Charles Mingus: More than a Fakebook (Hal Leonard)
Mingus website: www.mingusmingusmingus.com

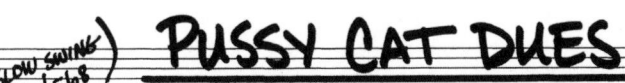

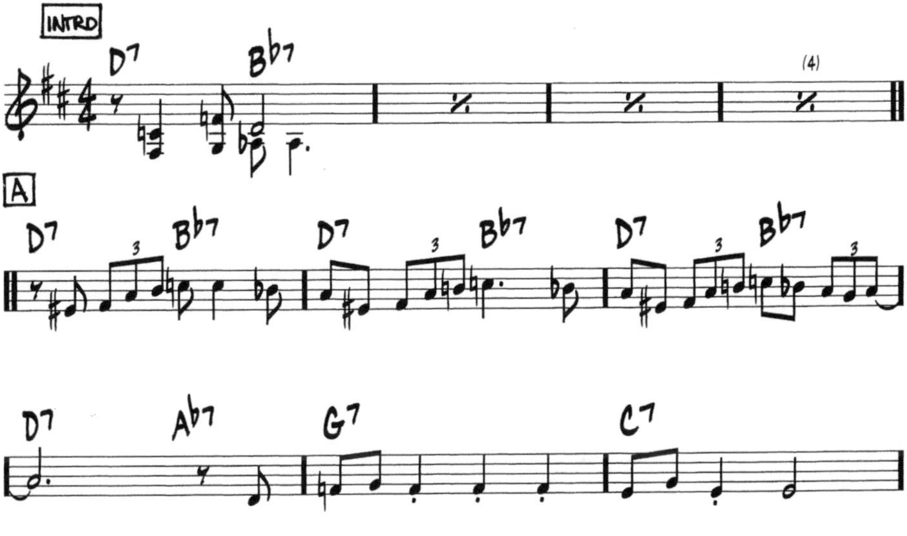

Copyright © 1975 (Renewed 2003) JAZZ WORKSHOP, INC.

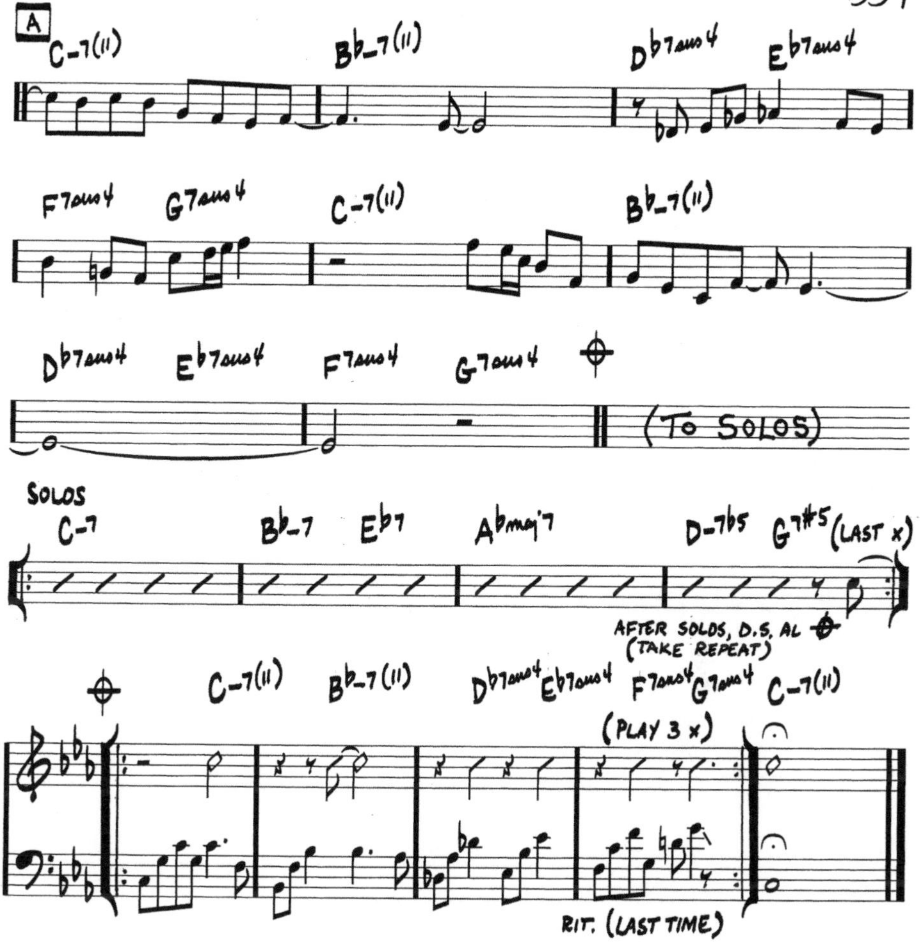
A
C-7(11)
Bb-7(11)
Db7sus4
Eb7sus4
F7sus4
G7sus4
C-7(11)
Bb-7(11)
Db7sus4
Eb7sus4
F7sus4
G7sus4
(TO SOLOS)
SOLOS
C-7
Bb-7
Eb7
Abmaj7
D-7b5
G7#5
(LAST x)
AFTER SOLOS, D.S. AL
(TAKE REPEAT)
C-7(11)
Bb-7(11)
Db7sus4
Eb7sus4
F7sus4
G7sus4
C-7(11)
(PLAY 3 x)
RIT. (LAST TIME)

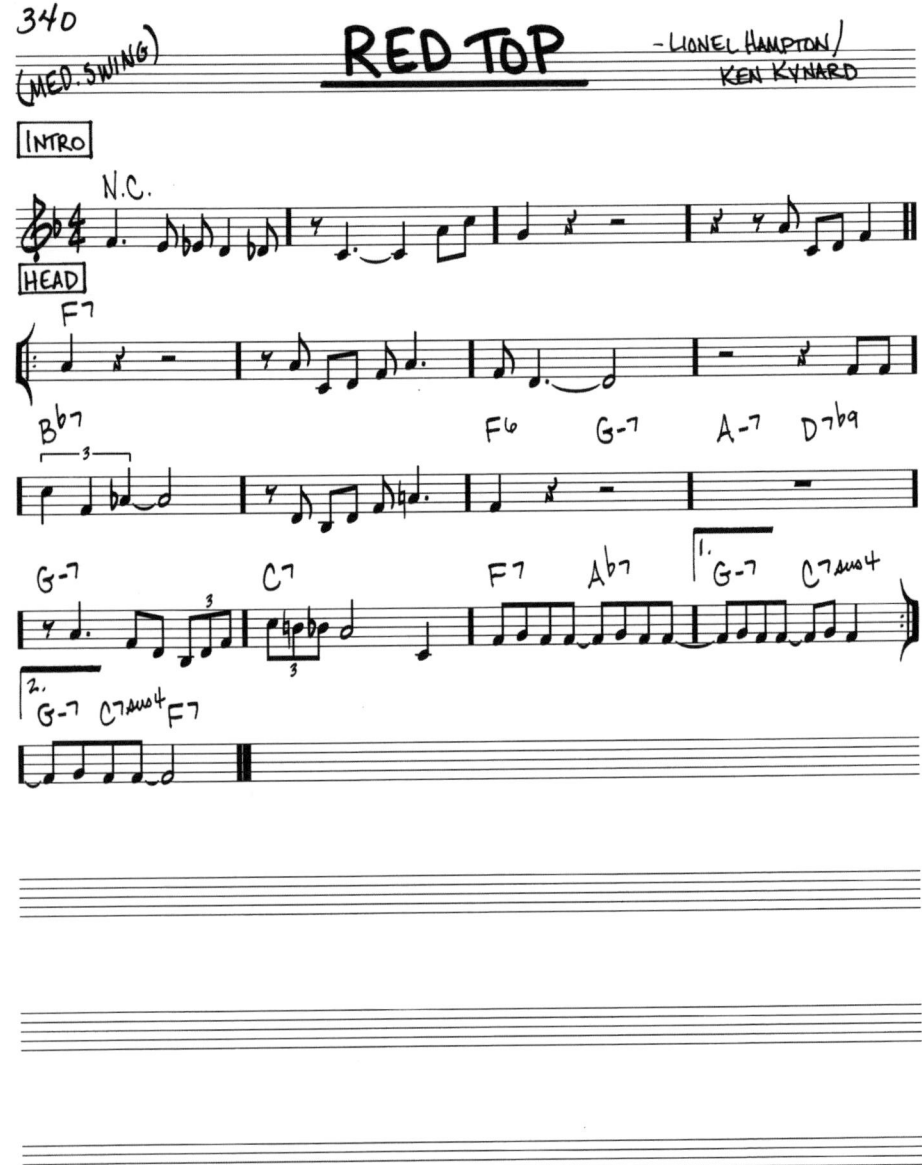

THE SAGA OF HARRISON CRABFEATHERS

—Steve Kuhn

(Jazz Waltz)

SATIN DOLL

-DUKE ELLINGTON

(MED.)

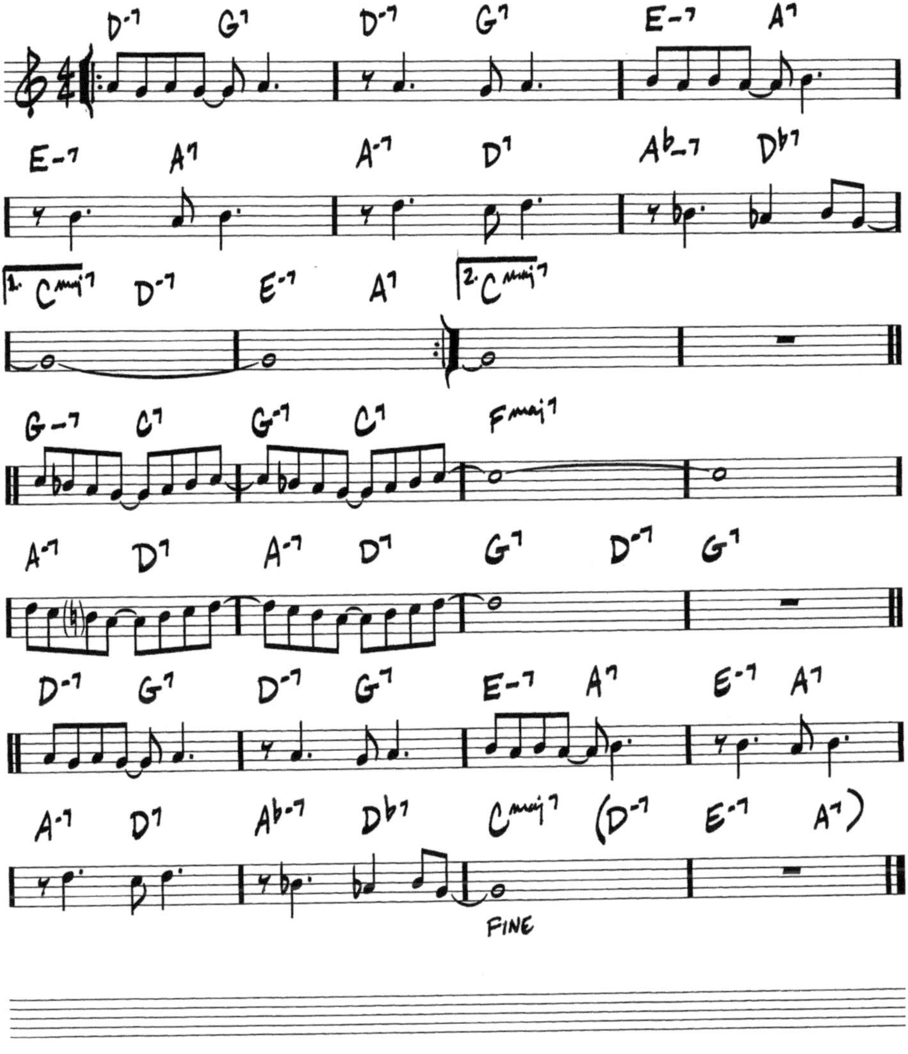

Copyright © 1953 (Renewed 1981) and Assigned to Famous Music Corporation in the U.S.A.
Rights for the world outside the U.S.A. Controlled by Tempo Music, Inc. c/o Music Sales Corporation

SEA JOURNEY

— Chick Corea / Neville Potter

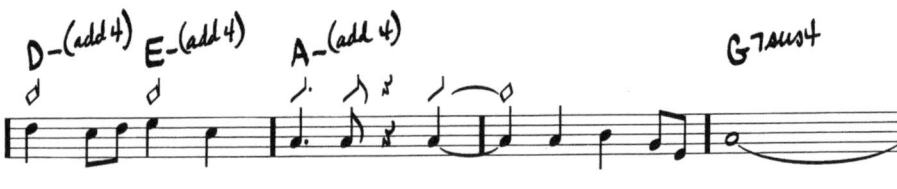

Copyright © 1972 UNIVERSAL MUSIC CORP.
Copyright Renewed

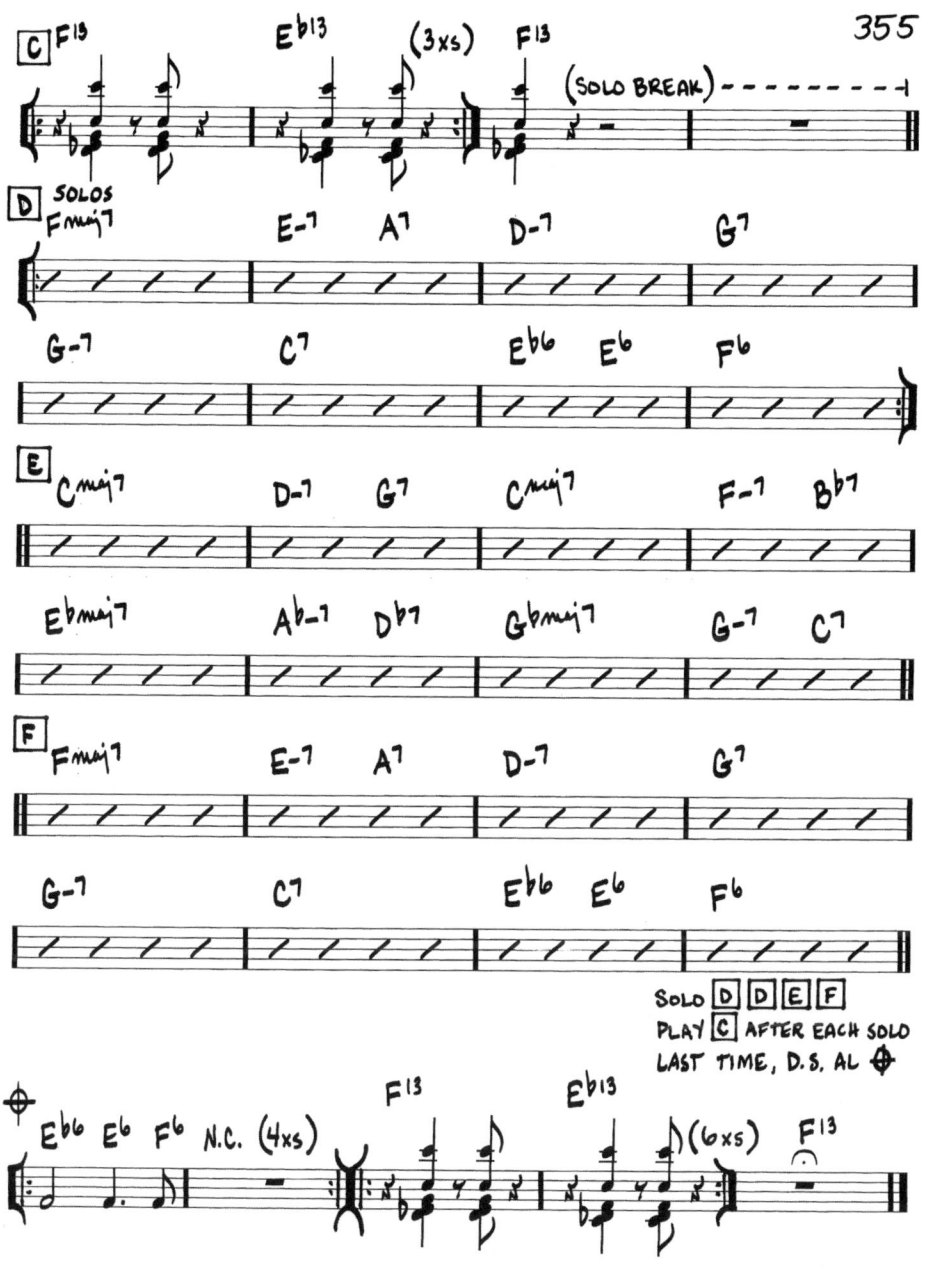

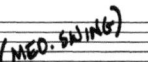

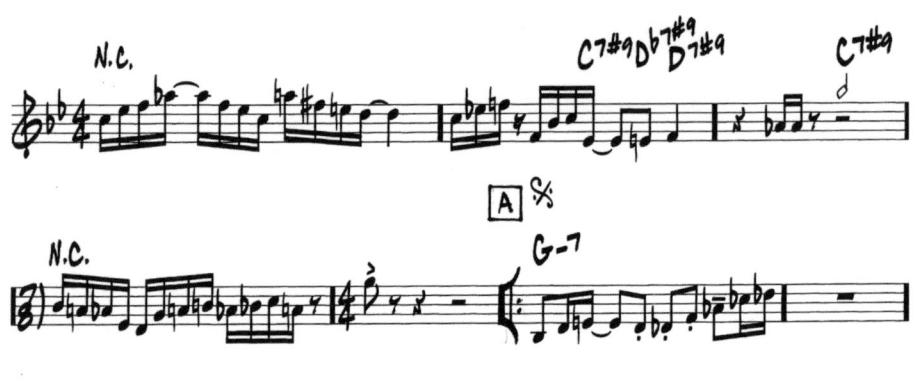

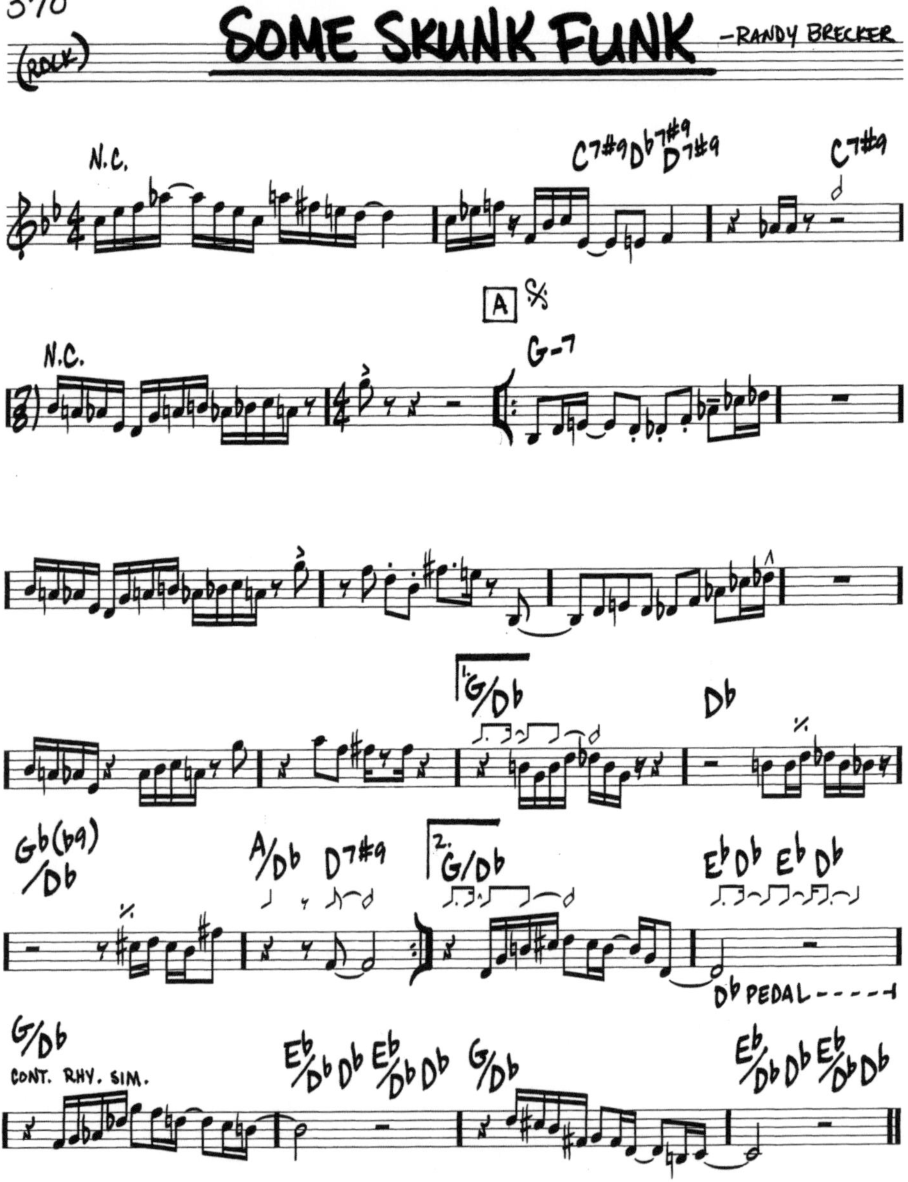

Copyright © 1975 (Renewed) Bowery Music (BMI)

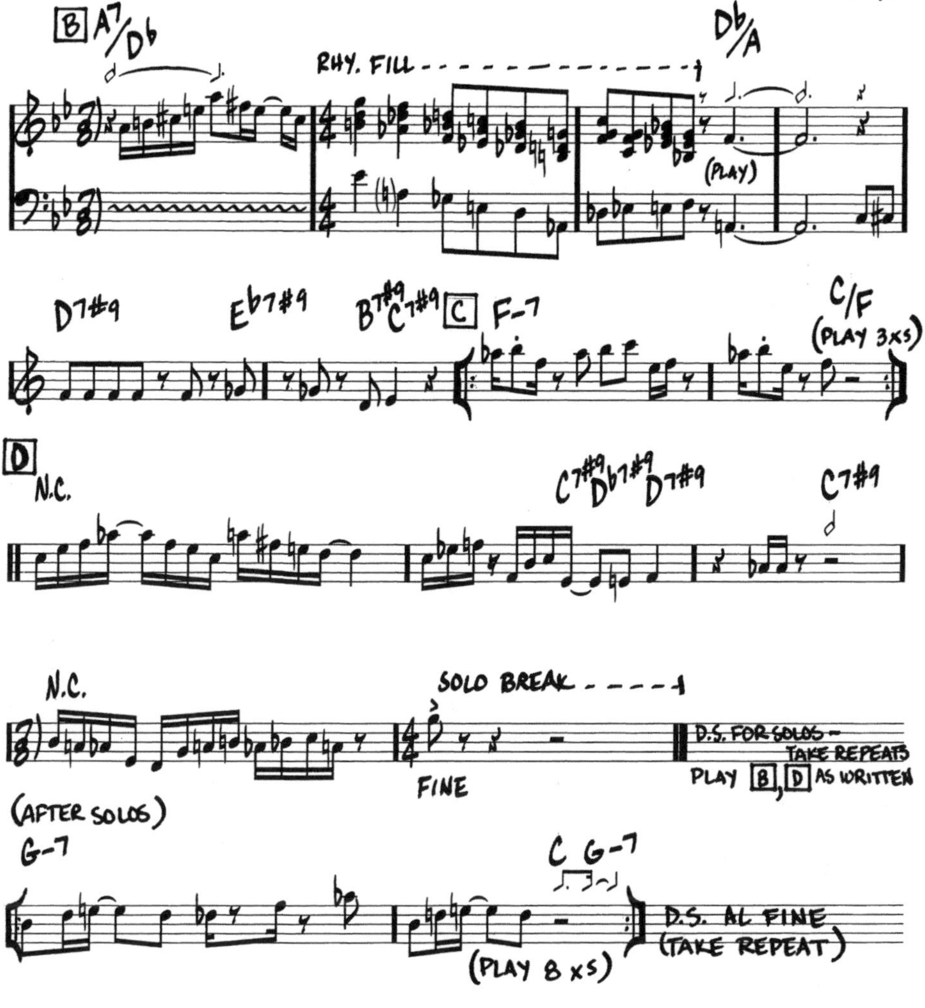
B
A7/Db
RHY. FILL
Db/A
(PLAY)
D7#9
Eb7#9
B7#9
C7#9
C
F-7
C/F
(PLAY 3XS)
D
N.C.
C7#9
Db7#9
D7#9
C7#9
N.C.
SOLO BREAK
FINE
D.S. FOR SOLOS -
TAKE REPEATS
PLAY B, D AS WRITTEN
(AFTER SOLOS)
G-7
C G-7
(PLAY 8 XS)
D.S. AL FINE
(TAKE REPEAT)

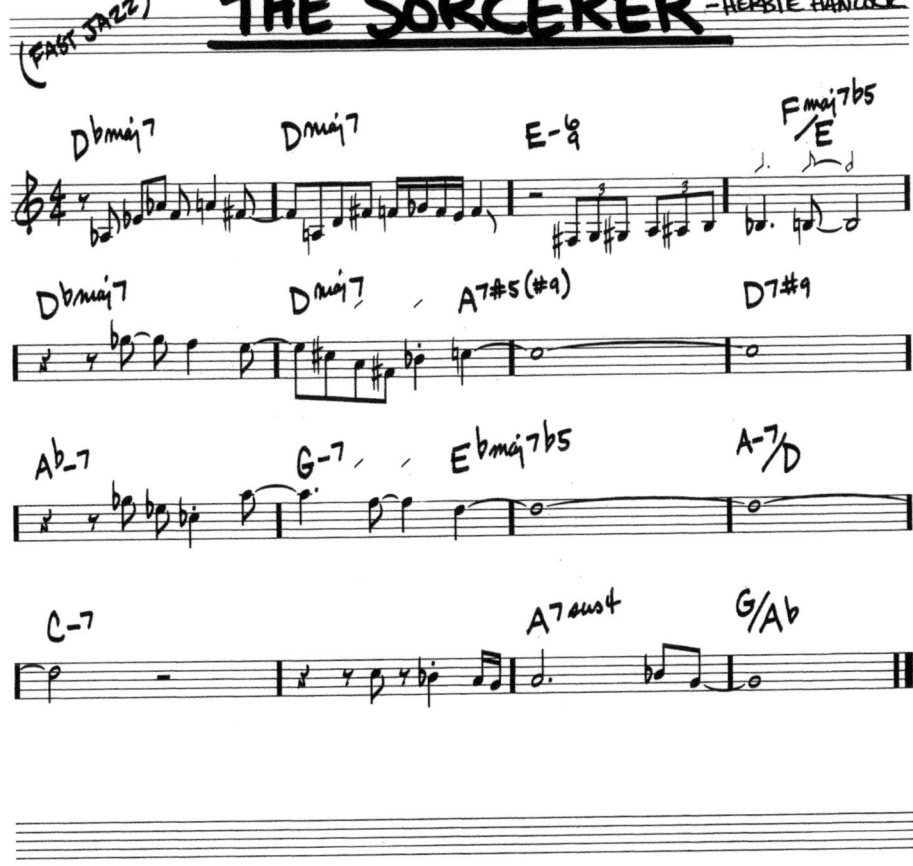

STEPS

(FAST JAZZ)

— CHICK COREA

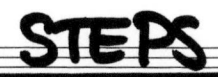

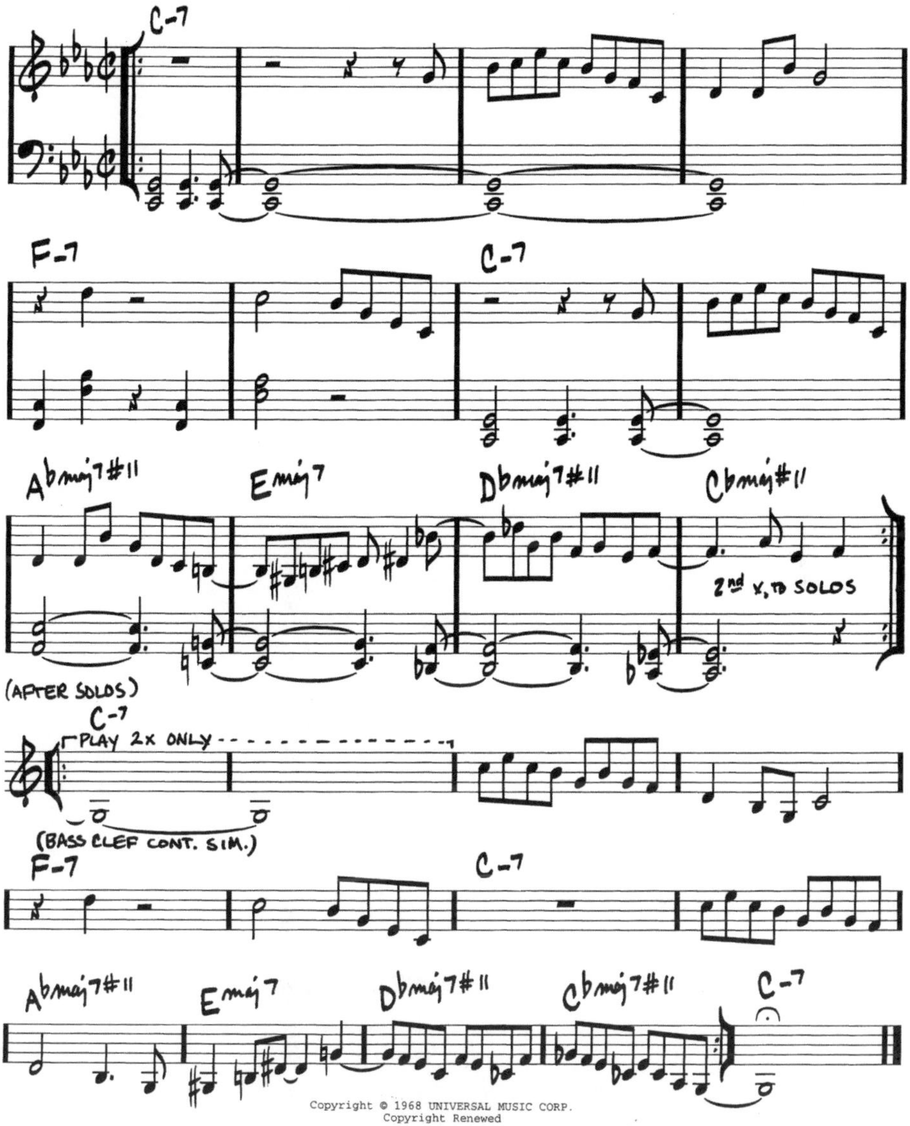

Copyright © 1968 UNIVERSAL MUSIC CORP.
Copyright Renewed

A Sunday Kind of Love

(MED.)

— Barbara Belle / Louis Prima / Anita Leonard / Stan Rhodes

THANKS FOR THE MEMORY

(MED.)

Leo Robin / Ralph Rainger

399

Copyright © 1937 (Renewed 1964) by Paramount Music Corporation

B7sus4 A7sus4 G#-7 E-7
Db-7 Eb-7 E-7 F#-7
Gmaj7(#11) F#-7
E-7 A7 Dmaj7 Cmaj7(#11) Bmaj7
*(Bmaj7) Gmaj7 Emaj7 Cmaj7(#11) Bmaj7 Gmaj7 Emaj7 Cmaj7
* RHYTHM AS BEFORE
AFTER SOLOS, D.S. AL
(ENDING VAMP)
(Emaj7) Cmaj7 Bmaj7 Gmaj7 Emaj7 Cmaj7 Bmaj7
(LAST X)

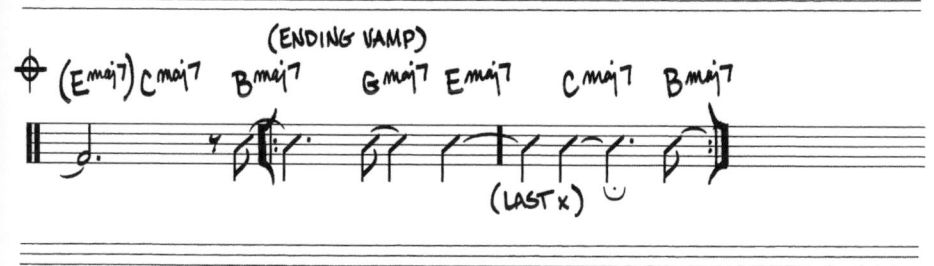

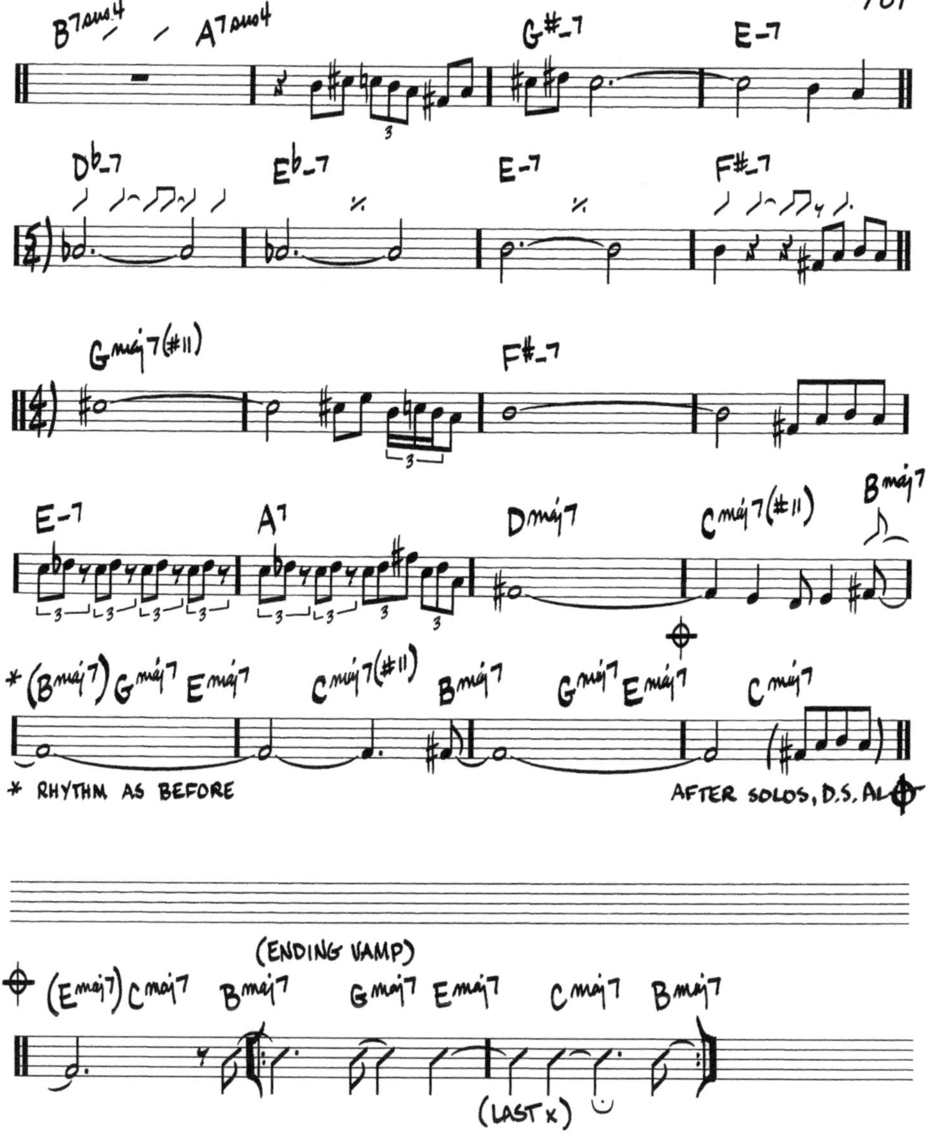

That's Amore (That's Love)

— Harry Warren / Jack Brooks

(Med.)

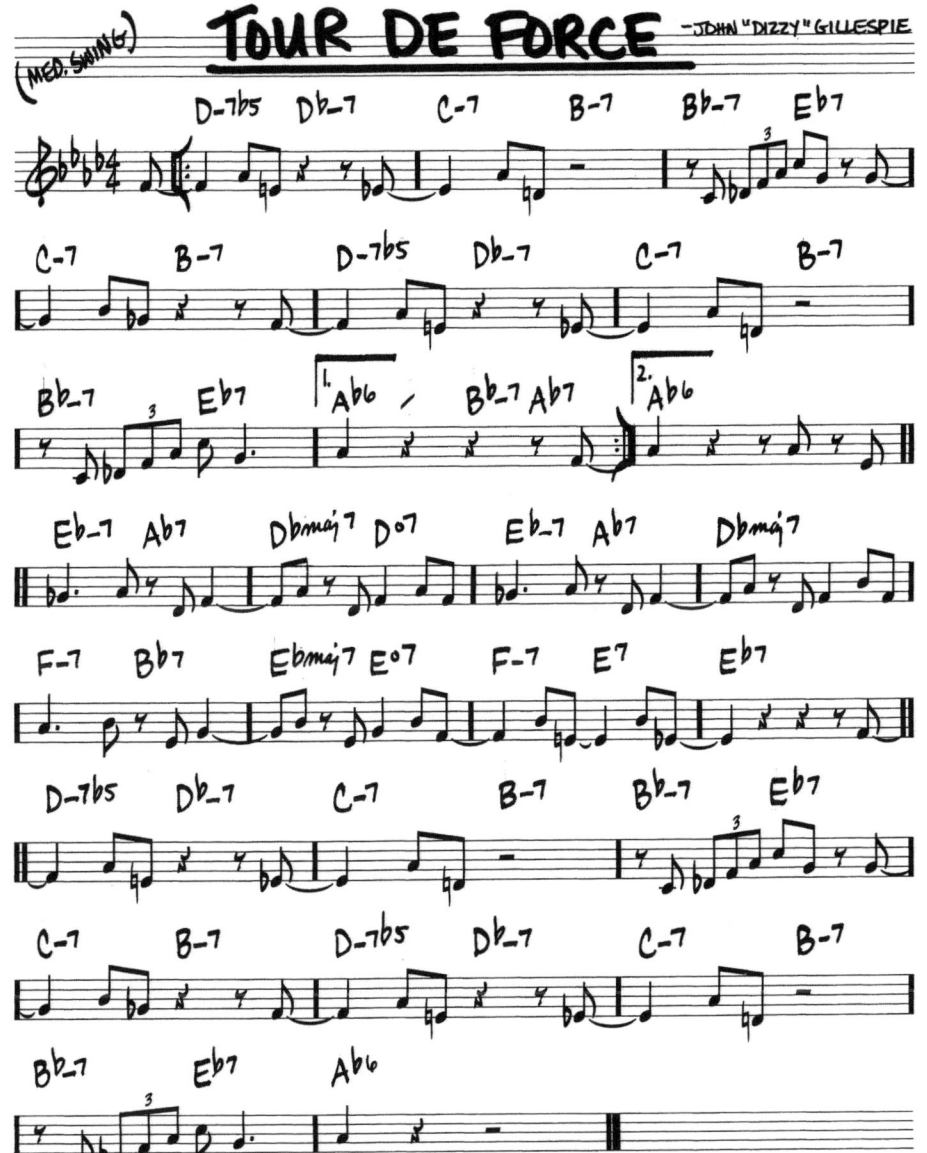

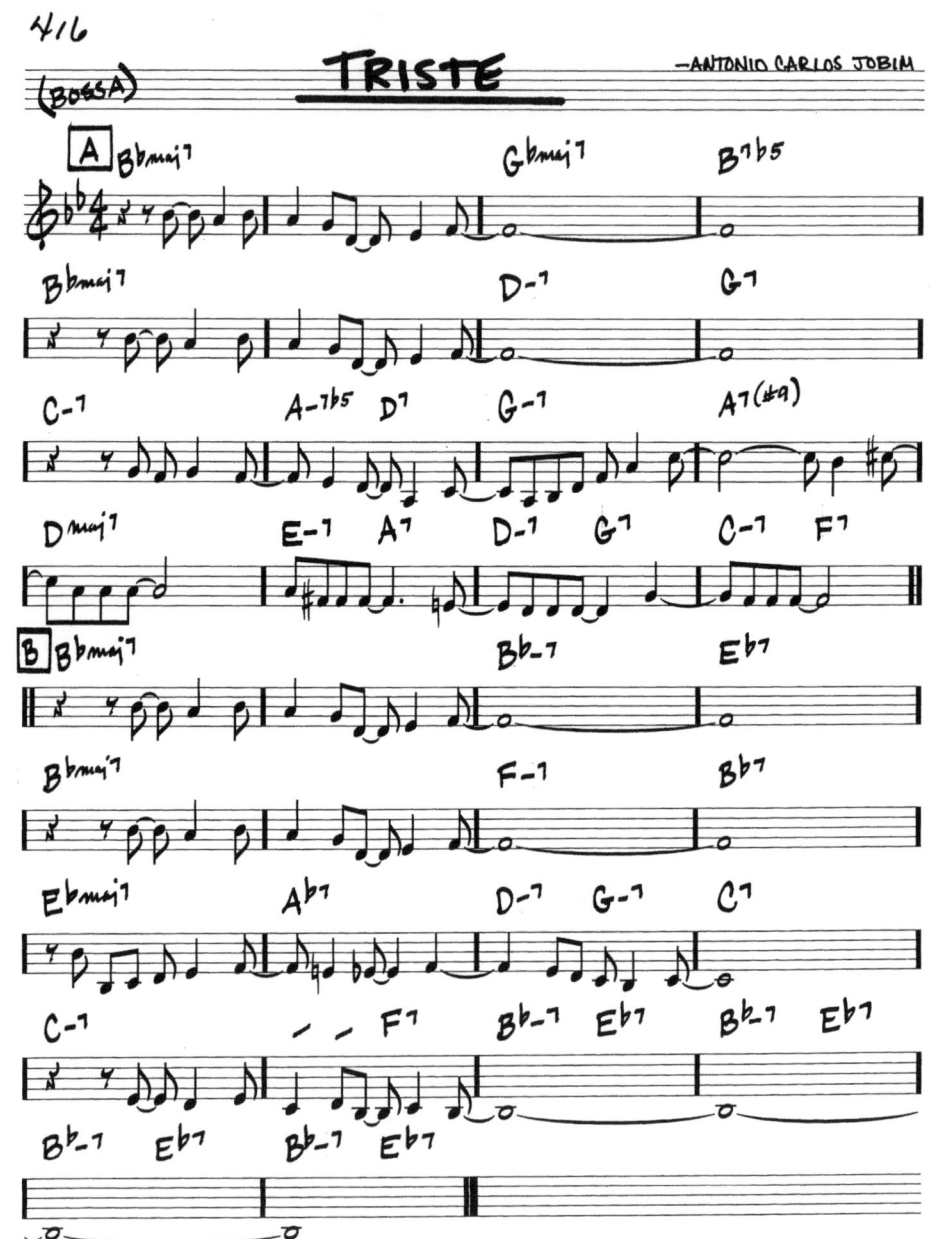

TUNE UP

-MILES DAVIS

(FAST BOP)

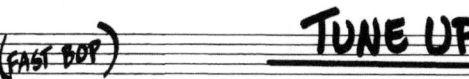

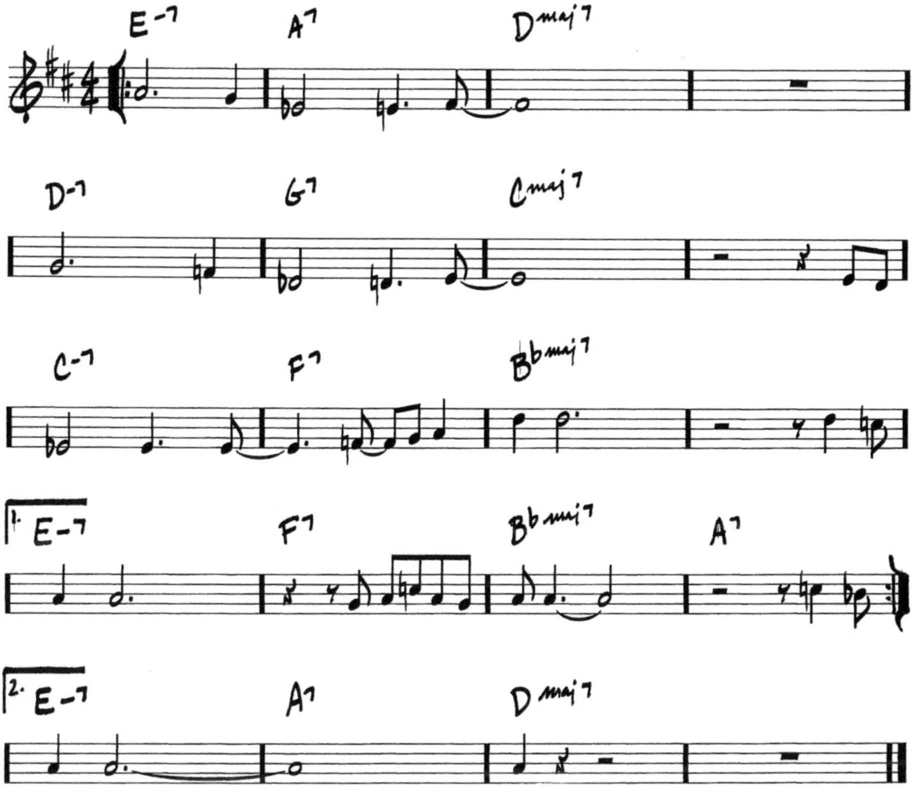

Copyright © 1963 Prestige Music
Copyright Renewed

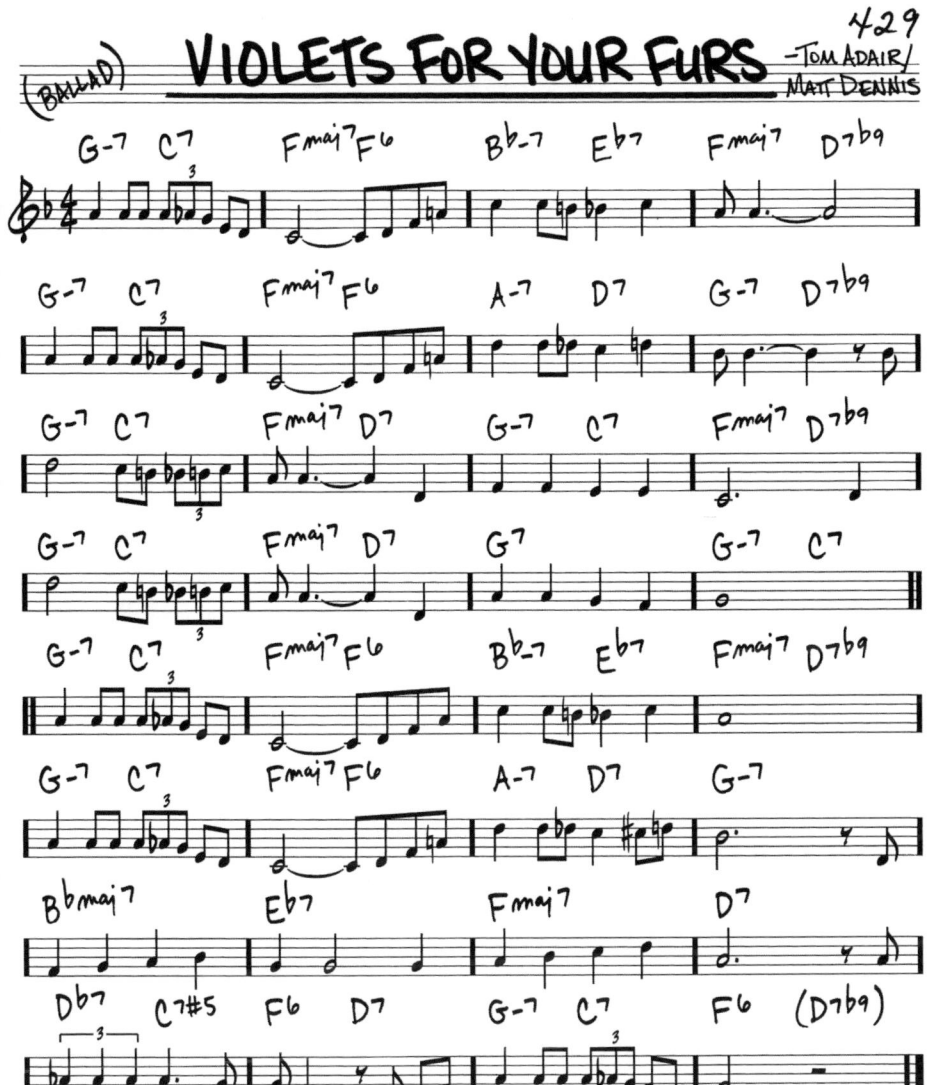

WATERMELON MAN

(MED. ROCK)

-HERBIE HANCOCK

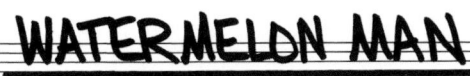

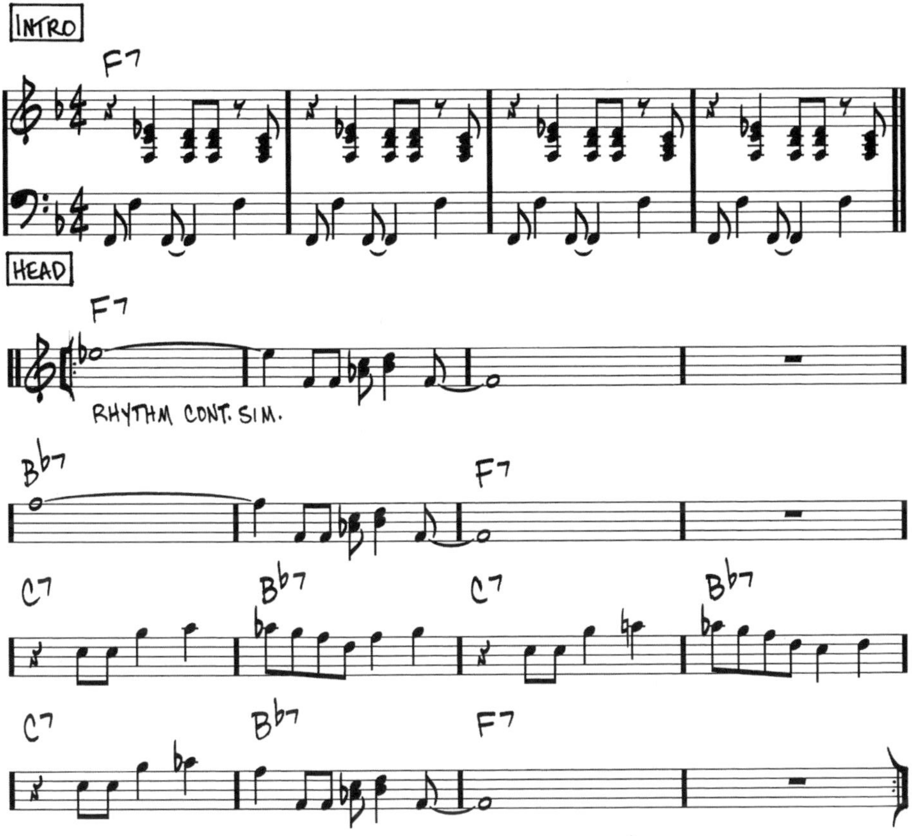

Copyright © 1973 (Renewed) by Hancock Music (BMI)

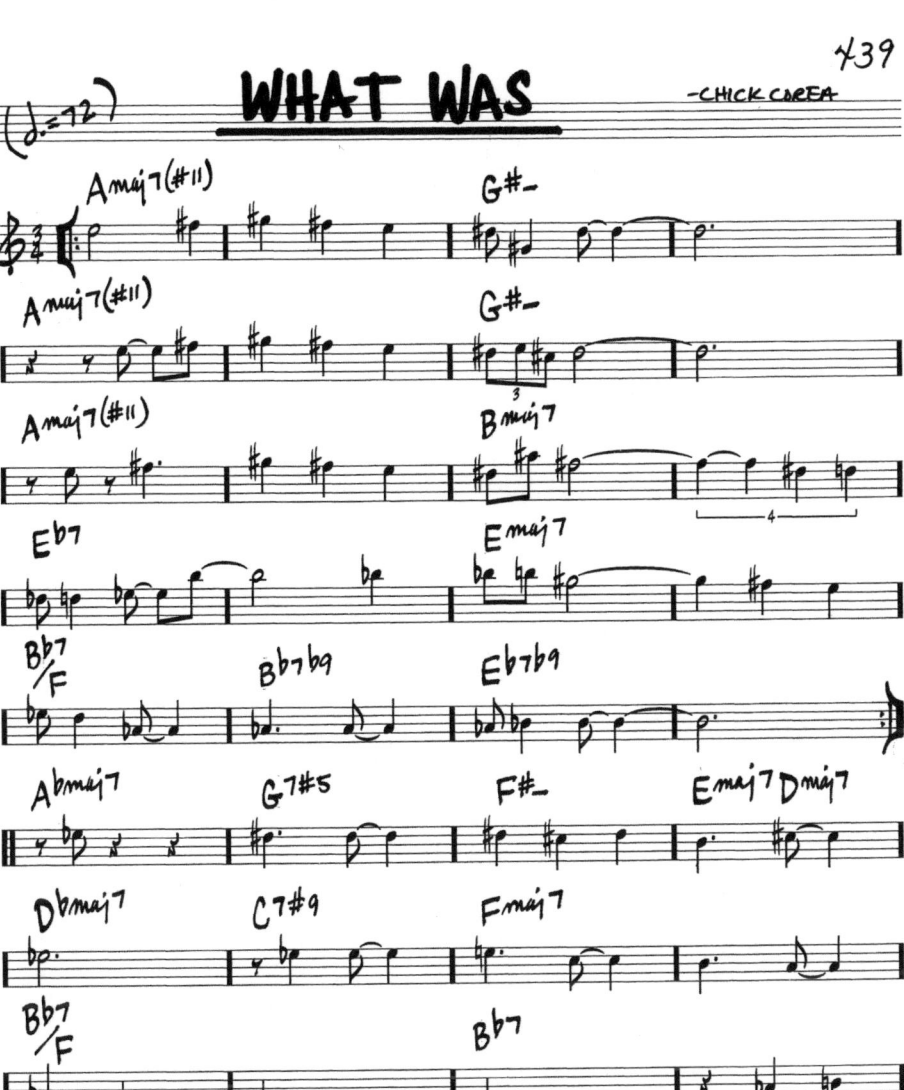

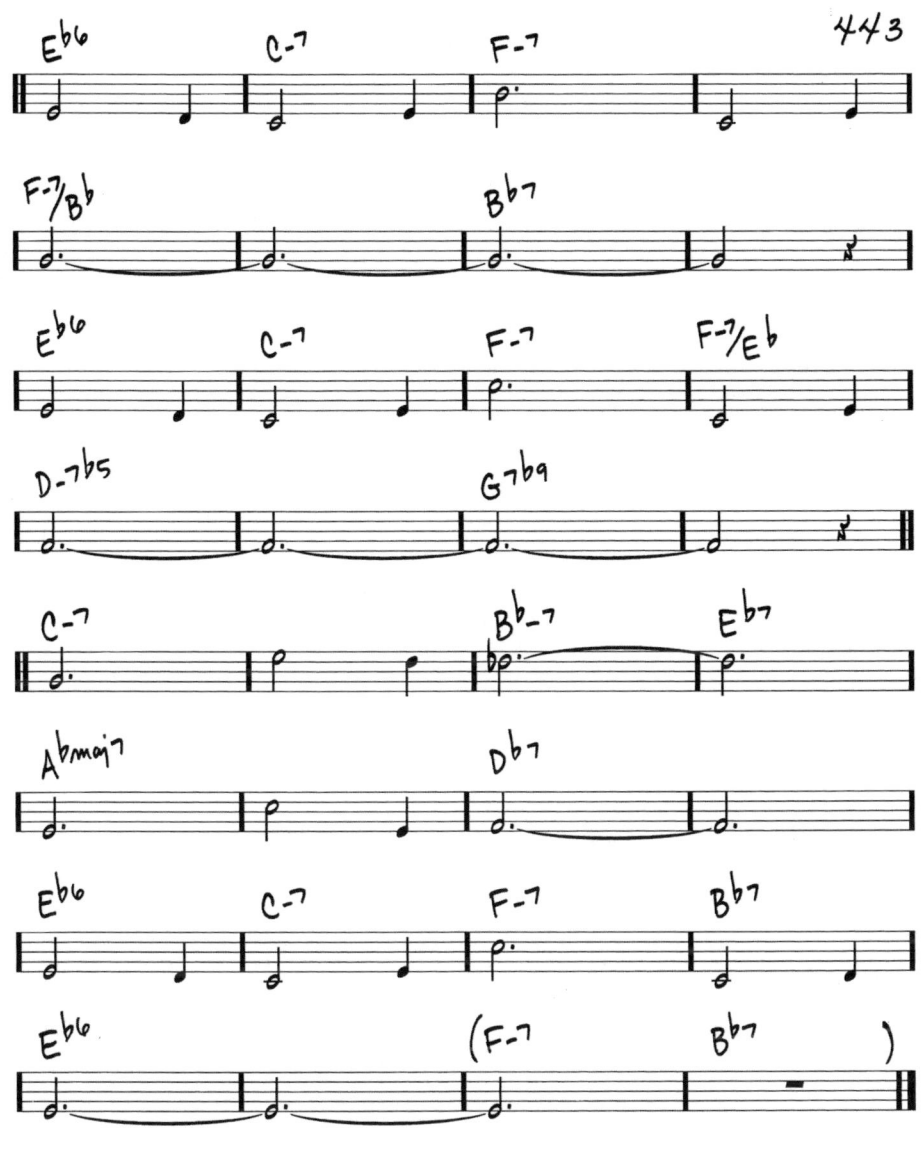

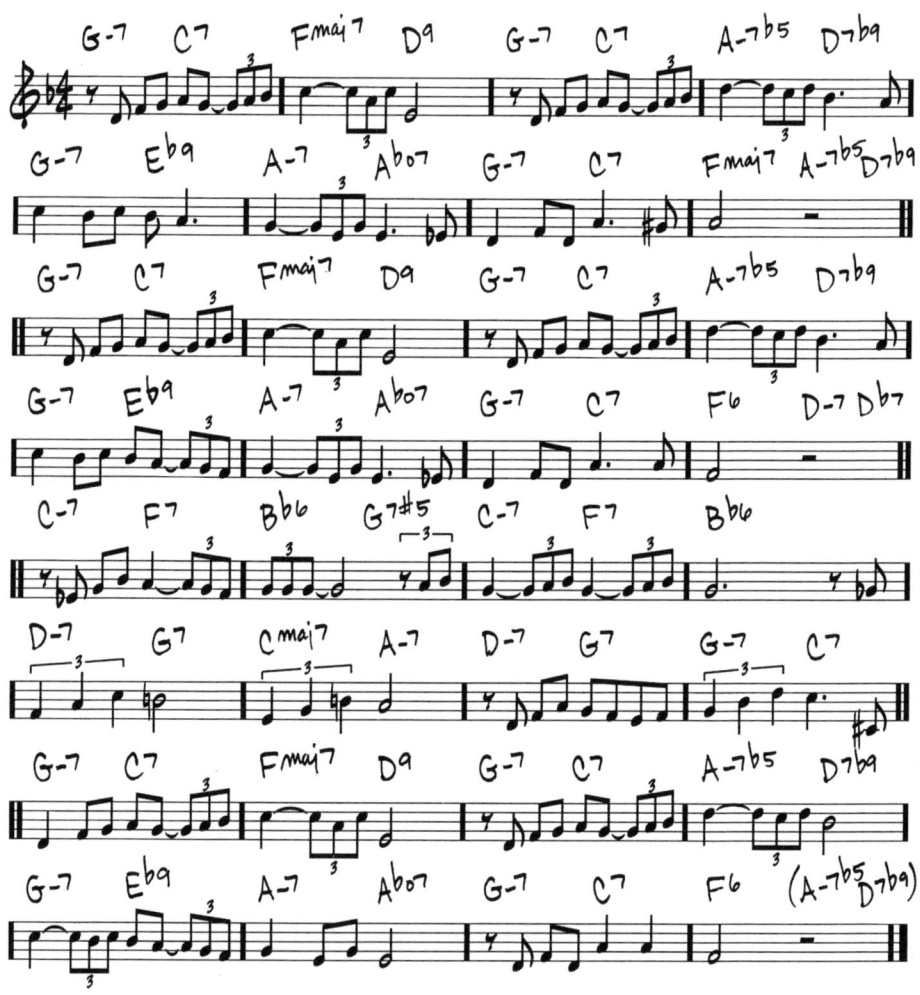

WINDOWS
— Chick Corea

Wives and Lovers
(Hey, Little Girl)

(Med. Jazz Waltz)

Burt Bacharach / Hal David

YES INDEED
— Sy Oliver

(MED. GOSPEL)